Jesus: The Strategic Life and Mission of the Messiah and His Movement—Volume 1: A Handbook

Experience the Gospels in a way you never imagined, and encounter Jesus, not as a distant religious figure, but as a master strategist, a revolutionary leader, and the architect of an insurgency that reshaped the world. This is not the domesticated Jesus of stained glass and sentimental sermons. This is the tactical genius who outmaneuvered empires, exposed religious corruption, and launched a movement that would shake history to its core.

This volume is your strategic guide to the messianic campaign of Jesus of Nazareth. More than just a retelling of events, it reconstructs Jesus' mission as a deliberate and calculated offensive—mobilizing followers, confronting opposition, and forcing a showdown with the rulers of his age. By treating the Gospels as a campaign dossier, *Jesus: The Strategic Life and Mission of the Messiah and His Movement—Volume 1: A Handbook* reveals the key moments of his insurgency: the early groundwork, the tactical retreats, the bold offensives, and the ultimate victory that defied both Rome and the grave.

This is not another abstract theological study. This is a field manual for understanding how Jesus waged war against the dominion of Sin, Death, and the oppressive powers of his world. With cutting-edge historical insights, sharp political analysis, and an unflinching commitment to the Bible's portrayal of Jesus, this book strips away centuries of misconceptions to reveal the revolutionary heart of his mission.

Through an immersive, chronological approach, this volume reconstructs Jesus' life as a series of strategic moves—each one designed to expose, undermine, and overthrow the corrupt systems that enslaved humanity. His campaign was not one of brute force, but of subversion, sacrifice, and ultimate triumph.

Whether you think you know Jesus or are just beginning to explore his story, this book will challenge your assumptions, deepen your understanding, and redefine your view of the Messiah who not only changed history but continues to call us to join his movement today.

This is Jesus' campaign. This is his revolution. Are you ready to join him?

Jesus: The Strategic Life and Mission of the Messiah and His Movement
Volume 1: A Handbook

A Guide for Studying the Gospels
Chronologically, Geographically, and Strategically
with Notes and Insights

Dr Tyson Putthoff

HEKHAL PUBLISHING CO.

Hekhal Publishing Co.

Hekhal Publishing Co. is dedicated to producing works that bridge the gap between academic scholarship and practical application, offering fresh, cutting-edge perspectives on biblical studies, theology, and the ancient world. Our mission is to make complex ideas accessible, engaging, and transformative.

For more information, visit: https://www.hekhal.co

First published 2025

AUTHOR: Tyson Putthoff
Jesus: The Strategic Life and Mission of the Messiah and His Movement, Volume 1: A Handbook | Includes bibliographical references

LCCN: 2025937939
ISBN (paperback): 979-8-9985268-0-0
ISBN (ebook): 979-8-9985268-1-7

HEKHAL PUB. CO. CID: 32819-00553

SUBJECTS: Jesus Christ; Gospels; Historical Jesus; New Testament—Theology; Kingdom of God; Christian Discipleship

Set in Cambria and Calibri.

בריך אינון עניי דלכון מלכותא דאלהא

Brikh innun aniei, dilkhon Malkuta d'Elaha

Blessed are you who are poor, for yours is the Empire of God

Preamble to Jesus' Imperial Constitution
Spring 28 AD, Beside the Sea of Galilee
Galilean Dialect of Aramaic
Adapted from Luke 6:20

When I first heard Dr Tyson Putthoff teach about the historical person of Jesus—at a public forum on the campus of Oklahoma State University in 2015—it felt like a light switch flipped on. Suddenly, the stories I'd known since childhood had new life and urgency. I grew up in an evangelical church, often hearing the call to "follow Jesus." But if I'm honest, it wasn't always clear how to do that. Beyond building community and inviting others in, I struggled to connect the dots between Jesus' world-changing message and my everyday life.

That's why this book is so powerful. Dr Putthoff takes us on a journey to discover "what Jesus did" in a way that is both deeply historical and incredibly practical. His insights help bridge the gap between ancient texts and modern living, offering a fresh perspective on what it truly means to live like Jesus today.

If you've ever wondered how Jesus' revolutionary life and message apply to your work, your relationships, or even the way you see the world—this book is for you. Prepare to be challenged, inspired, and equipped to follow Jesus in ways that will make a real difference—not only in your life but in the lives of those around you.

Dr Marlin Blankenship
University Professor, Executive Coach,
Founder of Blankenship Coaching Co.

—NOTE FROM THE AUTHOR—

This book is the product of my own decades-long journey with the Jesus of the Gospels. From the bottom of my heart, I want to thank you for joining me on this journey, and it is my hope and prayer that this book will serve as a tool to take your own study of and relationship with Jesus to a level you never imagined possible.

Before you dive in, I want to offer some motivation—and perhaps some clarification—about why this series, and this book in particular, is necessary in the first place. Many Christian readers may feel uneasy approaching the Gospels through the lens of Jesus' revolutionary mission, as I emphasize here. It's common to dismiss such a reading as the "social gospel," as if it reduces Jesus' mission to worldly concerns (e.g., *merely* helping the poor, *just* changing social and political structures, or *only* reshaping religious systems) while neglecting his eternal purpose of defeating Sin, Death, and Chaos, and ensuring our salvation for eternity. But this creates an artificial divide—one that forces a choice between seeing Jesus as a spiritual savior or as a figure deeply engaged in the realities of this world.

The Gospels themselves do not present this as an either-or choice. Jesus' work encompassed both the eternal and the immediate, the heavenly and the earthly. He did not come merely to offer salvation in the afterlife. He came to inaugurate the Empire of God here and now, "on earth as it is in heaven"—to quote Jesus himself (Matthew 6:10). His mission was not just about securing individual souls for eternity, but about overthrowing the present world order and establishing a new reality rooted in justice, mercy, and self-giving love. Rather than a fatalistic view of the world as being irreparable, unfixable, doomed to a path of destruction until his return, Jesus had hope—he saw a way for humans to fix the world that God had originally called "good." Jesus believed that by changing our ways, by loving one another selflessly the way he loved us, life on earth would actually improve before his return. And he showed us in his own life and campaign how to bring about this change in the world. The Gospels record the path he laid out for us.

As you read this book, I invite you to set aside preconceived ideas and encounter Jesus anew. My hope is that you will see him both as the Savior of the world *and* as the brilliant strategist, leader, and architect of a movement that continues to turn the world upside down.

LEKH ULMAD—Go and Learn!

Tyson

—TABLE OF CONTENTS—

SECTION I—INTRODUCTION

Why This Series is Necessary

Since the moment the Son of God entered humanity as Jesus of Nazareth, he became and forever remains both fully divine and fully human. This is a foundational truth affirmed by the Bible and nearly two millennia of Christian tradition. Yet from early on, much of Christian thought has leaned heavily toward emphasizing Jesus' divinity while often neglecting his humanity. There has long been an unspoken fear that focusing too much on Jesus as a man would somehow diminish his status as God. But nothing could be further from the truth. In fact, failing to fully embrace Jesus' human side distorts the very core of his mission and message.

This three-volume series is designed to reclaim the full picture of Jesus—both his divinity and his humanity—and in doing so, to reveal his mission in its true depth. It challenges the tendency to reduce Jesus' purpose to either a purely spiritual salvation or a political movement. The reality is that Jesus' mission was both eternal and earthly, both cosmic and immediate. He did not come merely to prepare people for the afterlife—he came to inaugurate, in his own words, the Empire of God here and now, "on earth as it is in heaven" (Matthew 6:10). His work was not just about securing individual souls for eternity but about overthrowing the present world order and establishing a new civilization based on love, justice, and self-sacrifice.

Yet, for many Christian readers, approaching Jesus in this way may feel uncomfortable. It is common to dismiss this perspective as the "social gospel," as if recognizing the deeply political nature of Jesus' actions somehow undermines his role as the divine Savior. But this creates an artificial divide—one that forces a false choice between seeing Jesus as the Son of God who came to save humanity or as a figure deeply engaged in the realities of this world. The Gospels themselves do not present this as an either-or choice.

The truth is that Jesus was—and is—the rightful King of heaven and earth. His mission was a revolutionary movement in the truest sense. It was a direct challenge to every power structure that stood in opposition to God's rule—whether human or spiritual, religious or political, earthly or cosmic.

This is not an interpretation imposed onto the Gospels—it is embedded in the text itself. Consider three glaringly obvious facts from the life of Jesus that are undeniably central to the Gospels:

1. **Jesus was executed by crucifixion—a punishment reserved for political insurrectionists.** Rome did not crucify religious figures for their beliefs, even if they sought to establish a new religious movement. Crucifixion was a brutal punishment reserved for those who challenged imperial rule. Jesus knew this. He lived in a time when other self-proclaimed "messiahs" from Galilee attempted to overthrow Rome and were swiftly crushed. The fact that Jesus died in this manner tells us how both Rome and the religious authorities perceived him—not as a mere teacher, but as a threat to their power.
2. **The titles "Lord" and "Messiah" were deeply political.** Today, we often use these terms in purely religious ways, but in Jesus' time, "Lord" was a title for rulers, including Caesar himself, and "Messiah" evoked the expectation of a kingly figure who would liberate Israel. Many of Jesus' contemporaries assumed he was another revolutionary leader like the Maccabees, one who sought to overthrow Rome.
3. **Jesus' central proclamation—the "Kingdom of God" (or, as I call it, the "Empire of God")—was an inherently political message.** In a world where Caesar ruled and claimed divine status, for Jesus to announce the arrival of God's reign was a direct challenge to the prevailing order. His teachings, parables, and miracles were not just moral lessons or spiritual metaphors; they were acts of defiance against a system that oppressed the poor, exploited the vulnerable, and distorted God's justice.

To read the Gospels without recognizing this reality is to miss the full weight of Jesus' challenge—not just to Rome and the religious elite, but to the very powers of Sin, Death, and Chaos that he came to overthrow.

So why does this matter? The implications are enormous.

First, Jesus had to be human for his work of salvation to be complete. The Bible makes clear that his ability to save humanity was directly tied to his full participation in human life (Hebrews 2:17). His mission wasn't just about offering a divine rescue plan—it was about stepping fully into human weakness, temptation, and suffering in order to redeem us from within.

Second, the Son of God did not become human merely out of necessity—he chose to. He took on flesh because he wanted to— because his love for us was so deep that he chose to share in our suffering, our struggles, and even our shame. He did not remain distant, untouched by the human experience. Instead, he fully entered into it, making himself relatable, accessible, and intimately connected to our reality.

Third, Jesus' life itself was a blueprint for how we are called to live. If we only emphasize his divinity, we risk treating him as an unreachable figure, a distant God who came simply to perform miracles and die for our sins. But if we take his humanity seriously, we recognize that his actions, strategies, and decision-making show us how to follow him.

With all this in mind, this series is written to highlight three essential truths:

1. **Jesus is far more relatable than we often think.** He experienced hunger, exhaustion, rejection, grief, and anger. He navigated friendships, betrayal, and the struggles of daily life. Seeing Jesus in his full humanity deepens our connection to him in profound ways.

2. **Jesus' brilliance as a strategist is often overlooked.** Having set aside his divine powers, he carried out his mission not through supernatural shortcuts but through extraordinary wisdom, careful planning, and a radical yet calculated approach to changing the world. His movements, his confrontations, his teachings, and even his final sacrifice were all part of a deliberate strategy. This series explores the sheer genius of how he carried out his messianic campaign.

3. **If we only focus on Jesus' divinity, we miss his true calling for us.** Christianity has often reduced Jesus' mission to a purely spiritual endeavor: he came, he died, he saved us so that we could go to heaven. But this narrative, while containing truth, ignores the actual life of Jesus and what the Gospels reveal about his purpose. His mission was not just about getting people to "believe" in him—it was about calling people to "follow" him.

And there's a big difference.

When we see Jesus only as a divine Savior who secures our place in heaven, we reduce the Gospels to a collection of important teachings with no direct bearing on our daily lives. Our faith becomes passive—we "believe" in Jesus, but we don't necessarily follow him.

But Jesus wasn't just preaching about the afterlife. He was bringing heaven to earth. He was establishing a new Empire, a new civilization—one built on love, self-sacrifice, justice, and the complete overthrow of Sin, Death, and Chaos.

To take Jesus' humanity seriously means to take his life and mission seriously. The Gospels aren't just stories about what he said and did—

they are a campaign dossier, a strategic record of how he brought about a radical transformation in the world. Jesus did not wander aimlessly through Galilee and Judea. He moved with precision, with intent. He infiltrated hostile territories, confronted corrupt leadership, gathered followers, trained them, and built a movement that would outlast Rome itself.

When we recognize this, we realize that Jesus' life is not just something to believe in—it's something to step into. We are not just called to admire him but to join his movement. Because the Gospel is not just the good news that Jesus saves *in the future.* It is the good news that Jesus reigns *even at this moment.* And that we, too, are called to take part in the victory of his Empire—here and now.

What This Handbook Is About

This handbook is the first of three volumes exploring the life and messianic campaign of Jesus. It serves as a tactical guide to his mission, presenting his movements in a clear, structured, and chronological framework. Rather than viewing the Gospels merely as theological reflections or moral teachings, this volume approaches them as a campaign record—a strategic account of how Jesus mobilized his movement, engaged with both religious and political authorities, and established the Empire of God in the face of overwhelming opposition.

Jesus' mission was not random or improvised. Every decision— where he traveled, whom he confronted, when he retreated—was deliberate. He was not merely a preacher of religious truths but a revolutionary leader executing a carefully orchestrated offensive against the forces of Sin, Death, and Chaos, along with their earthly proxies in governments, religious institutions, and oppressive systems.

This handbook systematically traces Jesus' campaign through 28 strategic scenes, divided into six phases, reflecting the evolution of his mission. Each scene includes:

- **Campaign Chronology**—A structured timeline of Jesus' movements, tracking his strategic advances across Galilee, Judea, and beyond.
- **Contextual Analysis**—Historical, political, and religious insights into the forces shaping his mission.
- **Strategic & Tactical Insights**—A closer look at how Jesus advanced his campaign, outmaneuvered his opponents, and laid the foundation for his Kingdom.

- **Key Questions for Reflection**—Encouraging deeper engagement with the implications of Jesus' actions and their relevance today.

What This Handbook Includes

More than a timeline, this handbook is a strategic report on Jesus' life, revealing the calculated acts, bold offensives, and tactical retreats that defined his campaign. By integrating historical context, political realities, and military-style strategy, it offers a fresh perspective on his mission.

Inside, you'll find:

- **A Fully Mapped Chronology**—Jesus' movements meticulously tracked through the four Gospels, showing his strategic decisions, retreats, and calculated advances.
- **Geopolitical & Military Context**—How Jesus navigated Roman occupation, Jewish revolutionary movements, and Herodian rule, positioning himself as a disruptor.
- **Climate & Terrain Factors**—How seasonal weather, geography, and ancient infrastructure shaped his travel, the spread of his message, and the risks of his campaign.
- **Key Strategic Questions**—Insights into why Jesus chose specific locations, engaged (or avoided) certain confrontations, and timed his actions for maximum impact.
- **Jewish Messianic Expectations**—How Jesus subverted prevailing ideas of the Messiah, challenging both Rome and the Jewish elite while redefining kingship and divine authority.
- **Tactical Moves & Parables as War Rhetoric**—Jesus' parables, miracles, and public debates analyzed not just as moral lessons, but as covert calls to allegiance within his movement.
- **Rome's Perception of Jesus as a Threat**—Why Pilate deemed Jesus dangerous enough to execute, and how his movement fit within Rome's pattern of crackdowns on insurrectionists.
- **A Ground-Level Perspective on Jesus' Life**—A boots-on-the-ground reconstruction of how Jesus and his followers navigated daily life amid taxation, oppression, and shifting alliances.
- **People, Places, and Cultural Insights**—Essential descriptions of key figures, locations, and concepts that shaped Jesus' world, providing deeper historical and contextual background.

Whether you're a scholar, student, or follower of Jesus, this handbook will challenge you to see the Gospels not just as stories, but as a strategic blueprint—a record of how Jesus built his movement and how we are called to follow in his steps.

How This Handbook is Divided

This handbook is structured to present Jesus' life and mission as a strategic campaign, mapping out his movements with precision and clarity. Following this introductory section (Section I), you'll find yourself in the heart of this book: the chronological presentation of Jesus' life and mission (Section II). Here, Jesus' life is divided into six major "phases," each representing a key stage in his messianic offensive. These "phases" mark the broad shifts in strategy—from the early mobilization of his followers to his final confrontation in Jerusalem and ultimate victory over Sin, Death, and Chaos through the cross and resurrection. Each "phase" captures the overarching trajectory of his insurgency against the ruling powers, both human and cosmic.

Within these "phases" are twenty-eight "scenes," which highlight specific engagements, movements, and tactical shifts in Jesus' campaign. These "scenes" function as individual operations, each advancing his mission in a calculated way—whether by expanding his influence, challenging religious and political authorities, or preparing his disciples for the coming storm. Some "scenes" involve direct action, such as the cleansing of the Temple or his confrontations with the Pharisees, while others focus on strategic retreats, key teachings, or significant turning points in his movement.

At the end of this handbook (Section III), you'll find supplemental material that provides essential background for understanding the Gospels and Jesus' world. These sections explore the historical, cultural, and political landscape of first-century Judea, offering critical insights into the figures, locations, and themes that shaped Jesus' campaign. This final section ensures that readers not only follow the strategic arc of Jesus' mission but also grasp the deeper context and implications of his revolutionary movement.

How to Use This Handbook

This handbook is designed to serve as a guide to the life of Jesus, offering both a chronological roadmap and a strategic analysis of his campaign. Whether you're a scholar, a student, or an interested reader, here's how to get the most out of this work:

- **Keep this Handbook Close to Your Bible**—While reading the Gospels, keep this handbook open. Here, you can find information and commentary on the biblical texts as you read the story of Jesus in chronological order.
- **Read the Gospels Chronologically Side-by-Side**—The four accounts provide different perspectives, emphasizing unique details that form a more complete picture of his strategy, teachings, and challenges. This handbook provides references to every single Gospel chapter and verse, aligning these chronologically so that you can read Jesus' story in chronological order and see these connections more clearly.
- **Follow Jesus' Campaign From Start to Finish**—The events of Jesus' life are presented in historical sequence, numbered according to the "scenes"—28 in total, divided into six "phases"—allowing you to see how his movement evolved, from its earliest mobilization to its climactic confrontation in Jerusalem.
- **Use the Strategic Notes**—Each numbered "scene" includes insights into climate and geography; social, religious, and political context; and strategic and tactical insights, helping you understand why Jesus made certain moves and how his actions fit within the larger historical setting.
- **Engage with Key Strategic Questions**—Throughout this handbook, key tactical and theological questions appear, inviting you to reflect on Jesus' decision-making and the revolutionary nature of his message.
- **Explore Connections to Additional Resources**—This handbook is the first volume in a three-volume work on Jesus published with **Hekhal Publishing Co.** (www.hekhal.co), which delve deeper into specific aspects of his mission, such as his role as a messianic disruptor, engagement with Rome, and redefinition of kingship.
- **Listen Along with the Podcast Series**—This work is directly tied to the podcast series by Dr Tyson Putthoff, *What the Bible Actually Says* (www.bibleactuallysays.com) where episodes will unpack key events, figures, and themes in historical and theological depth.
- **Apply the Insights Practically**—Whether for teaching, research, or personal study, this handbook provides a clear and structured approach to Jesus' life, challenging traditional assumptions and offering a more dynamic, historically-grounded perspective.

SECTION II—JESUS' LIFE & CAMPAIGN

MESSIANIC LIFE—PREPARATION PHASE
THE ARRIVAL OF THE KING & HIS HERALD | 3 BC–27 AD

The Seeds of Insurrection

Before any revolution, there is a moment of quiet preparation—when the pieces begin moving into place, unnoticed by the ruling powers. The preparation phase of Jesus' messianic campaign unfolds in secrecy, far from the courts of Rome or the high priest's chambers in Jerusalem. His arrival is no grand coronation but an infiltration—born into an oppressed people under the shadow of Herod's paranoia and Rome's dominance. Like all great insurgencies, his movement first germinates among the lowly: a Galilean village, a Judean hill country, a Bethlehem stable.

This phase sets the foundation for the dual battle ahead—against the corrupt earthly systems of power and against the cosmic forces of Sin, Death, and Chaos. John the Baptist, the king's herald, emerges from the wilderness as a firebrand prophet, declaring that the old order is doomed. Jesus himself is raised in obscurity, avoiding premature detection while growing into his role as the revolutionary king. But in the background, forces are already aligning—Rome tightens its grip, Herod hunts down rivals, and the spiritual realm stirs in anticipation of the coming war. The revolution has not yet begun, but the world is already shifting.

—SCENE 1—
THE BIRTH OF THE KING

Before Jesus' Birth & the Birth of John the Baptist | Galilee, Judean Hills | 3–2 BC

Campaign Chronology

- **Pre-humanity of Jesus** | Jn 1:1-18
- **Genealogy** | Mt 1:1-17 | Lk 3:23-38
- **Luke's Purpose for Writing** | Lk 1:1-4
- **John the Baptist's Birth Foretold** | Lk 1:5-25
- **Jesus' Birth Foretold** | Lk 1:26-38
- **Mary's Visit to Elizabeth** | Lk 1:39-56
- **Birth of John the Baptist** | Lk 1:57-79
- **John from Youth to Campaign** | Lk 1:80

Geographical Insight

The Judean Hills were a rugged, isolated region, perfect for fostering movements outside of the direct control of urban elites. The prophetic traditions of the wilderness shaped John's apocalyptic message, much like the Essenes at Qumran, who anticipated divine intervention against corruption.

Nazareth was a nowhere town in Galilee, a region often dismissed by Jerusalem's elite. This was insurgent territory, a region filled with nationalist fervor, anti-Roman sentiment, and memories of past revolts. It was an unlikely place for a Messiah, but a perfect place for an underground movement to take root.

Bethlehem, the City of David, was a politically loaded location, the site of a prophesied ruler (Micah 5:2). Jesus' birth here aligns him with the great kings of Israel, yet his arrival was not to a throne but a manger—an inversion of power that would define his mission.

Tactical Insight

Secrecy was a powerful tool. The most powerful revolutions often began in obscurity. Jesus' early life was spent far from Rome's watchful eye, ensuring he would not be identified as a political threat too soon. His concealment in Egypt, mirroring Israel's exile, strategically delayed his public emergence.

John the Baptist's upbringing within priestly circles would have granted him access to the inner workings of the Temple system. His rejection of Temple authority in favor of the wilderness suggests he was preparing for something radical—a direct challenge to the establishment.

Social, Religious & Political Context

The ruler of a kingdom of fear, Herod the Great was a Roman puppet king, ruling with brutality. His paranoia led to widespread executions, including his own sons. A rival king, especially one of Davidic descent, posed an existential threat to his fragile rule.

Augustus Caesar ruled the Roman Empire, and his governors ensured heavy taxation and military enforcement of order. The Jews longed for liberation, and whispers of messianic hope circulated among the oppressed.

The religious elite in Jerusalem who maintained control over the Jerusalem Temple had grown wealthy through alliances with Rome, enforcing heavy tithes and selling sacrificial animals at marked-up prices. A true Messiah would not only challenge Rome but also these Jewish collaborators.

Strategic Questions

1. Why was the Messiah's arrival hidden in plain sight? If he was destined to challenge the world's power structures, why did he come as a vulnerable child rather than a warrior king? His arrival in humility was a strategic inversion of power. God's Empire would not rise through conquest but through self-sacrifice. By coming as a helpless child, Jesus subverted expectations and ensured that only those with eyes to see would recognize his true identity.

2. What did it mean for the Messiah to be raised in Galilee, a land of rebels and revolutionaries, rather than in Jerusalem, the city of kings? Growing up in Galilee shaped Jesus into an outsider, giving him proximity to the oppressed and instilling a revolutionary edge to his mission. Unlike Jerusalem's elite, he was formed in a region known for resistance, making him a Messiah who stood with the marginalized rather than ruling from the top down.

3. How did Herod's paranoia about a baby Messiah reflect larger fears within the ruling class? Was this merely about personal power, or was there a deeper, cosmic battle already unfolding? Herod's massacre was more than political survival. It was an instinctive reaction to a threat greater than Rome itself. The rulers of this world, both human and spiritual, understood that this child would overturn their dominion, setting in motion a cosmic battle between the old order and the Empire of God.

4. What role did geography play in shaping John and Jesus? Would their missions have been the same if they had been raised in the centers of power rather than the margins of society? The wilderness bred prophets, not politicians—John's asceticism and Jesus' grassroots movement were shaped by their upbringing on society's fringes. Had they been raised in the halls of power, they might have become mere reformers of the system rather than catalysts of its overthrow.

—SCENE 2—
THE PREPARATION OF THE KING

Jesus' Birth, Childhood & Emergence | Nazareth, Bethlehem | 2 BC–27 AD

Campaign Chronology

- **Mary's Conception |** Mt 1:18
- **Joseph Encounters the Angel |** Mt 1:19-25
- **Jesus' Birth|** Lk 2:1-7

- **Shepherds Encounter the Angels** | Lk 2:8-20
- **Visit from the Magi** | Mt 2:1-12
- **Jesus' Circumcision, Presentation** | Lk 2:21
- **Jesus' Presentation in the Temple** | Lk 2:22-38
- **Flight to Egypt** | Mt 2:13-21
- **Return to Nazareth** | Mt 2:19-23 | Lk 2:39
- **Jesus' Childhood** | Mt 2:22-23 | Lk 2:40
- **The Boy Jesus in the Temple** | Lk 2:41-50
- **Jesus from Youth to Campaign** | Lk 2:51-52

Climate & Seasonal Context

If Jesus' birth aligns with winter, nights would be bitterly cold (35–45°F). Shepherds would only keep watch at night if necessary, meaning this was no ordinary season. An outdoor manger—typically a cave or a small stone enclosure—would be an exceptionally harsh place for a newborn.

Travel conditions were tough. Joseph and Mary's journey from Nazareth to Bethlehem (~90 miles) was arduous, with steep inclines, Roman roads built for military use rather than comfort, and constant threats from bandits. The Roman census dictated that travel had to be made despite conditions, reinforcing the oppressive weight of the Empire even in the most personal affairs.

Geographical Insight

Bethlehem was a small but historically significant town, the birthplace of King David and the prophetic focal point for messianic expectation (Micah 5:2). Rome's taxation policy and the census forced the Holy Family into this setting, unknowingly fulfilling divine prophecy.

Nazareth, an obscure Galilean village, was not mentioned in major historical texts of the period. It was a place of low status, certainly not the expected home of a world-altering king (John 1:46). Its remoteness protected Jesus from early political intrigue, allowing him to develop under the radar and launch his movement in his timing.

Social, Religious & Political Context

The Roman census of Quirinius was more than bureaucratic. It was a demonstration of Roman control over subjugated peoples. Forced registration underscored Jewish subservience to Caesar, making messianic expectations all the more potent.

Herod's massacre, the slaughter of Bethlehem's infants, was a classic Herodian move. It was a ruthless suppression of any perceived rival. Herod had already killed his own sons and wife to secure his throne. The murder of Jewish children fit his paranoid reign of terror. Jewish historian Josephus omits this specific event, but his accounts of Herod's cruelty affirm that such an act was entirely in character.

Tactical Insight

The flight to Egypt was a calculated retreat that mirrored Israel's historical journey in reverse. Jesus was hidden in enemy territory—Rome's breadbasket—but outside Herodian reach. This fulfilled Hosea 11:1 and positioned Jesus as a sort of new Moses, one who would return to liberate his people.

Growing up in Nazareth rather than Judea was a strategic move that kept Jesus away from the power centers of Jerusalem and Herodian influence. The Messiah was raised in obscurity, avoiding early detection while being prepared for his eventual campaign.

Strategic Questions

1. Why Bethlehem? It was both the city of David and a fulfillment of prophecy (Micah 5:2). Ironically, Rome's rule helped set the stage for prophecy to be realized.

2. Why an obscure beginning? Why not be born to a powerful family, or at least in Jerusalem? Jesus' rise from insignificance mirrors the insurgent nature of his entire movement, starting from the margins and overturning expectations.

3. Why retreat to Egypt? Why not confront Herod directly? This was not cowardice on the part of Joseph and Mary, but as it was divinely guided, it was instead the wisdom of living to fight another day—of allowing Jesus to live to adulthood to fulfill his divine mission.

4. Why return to Nazareth? Wouldn't it have been more strategic to grow up near the Temple, in the heart of Jewish religious and political power? Jesus' life and emergence in Galilee was pivotal not least because he launched his movement in a hotbed for revolutionary activity. Galileans were ready to revolt. They just didn't know how Jesus' revolution would actually look.

The Campaign Begins

Jesus' initial public activity was not that of a mere wandering preacher gathering followers. This was the calculated mobilization of an insurgency against the powers that ruled both earth and the unseen world. Jesus followed in the footsteps of John the Baptist, whose wilderness movement had already signaled rebellion against the corrupt establishment. Yet Jesus' mission went further. He was not merely calling for repentance. He was assembling forces, marking out enemy territory, and launching his first offensives.

The baptism and retreat into the wilderness was no act of passivity. It was a strategic withdrawal to prepare for war. His first public acts—selecting his closest followers, infiltrating synagogues, and striking at the Temple during Passover—were tactical moves designed to expose and undermine the ruling order.

By choosing Galilee, a region filled with anti-Roman sentiment and outside of direct Jerusalem control, as his operational base, Jesus ensured that his message spread rapidly while remaining beyond the immediate grasp of the religious and imperial authorities. He gathered his earliest converts from the margins—fishermen, tax collectors, and social outcasts—building an army of the overlooked and oppressed.

Each move in this phase was deliberate. Jesus' challenge to the Temple at the height of Passover was not an impulsive act of protest—it was the first signal of the revolution to come. The battle lines were being drawn. The Empire was advancing.

—SCENE 3—
THE MUSTERING OF FORCES

John the Baptist | Judean Desert, Jordan River Region | Late 26—Early 27 AD

Campaign Chronology

- **John's Campaign Inaugurated |** Mk 1:1 | Lk 3:1-2
- **John's Message & Appearance |** Mt 3:1-6 | Mk 1:2-6 | Lk 3:3-6
- **John versus Others |** Mt 3:7-10 | Lk 3:7-1
- **John's Description of the Messiah |** Mt 3:11-12 | Mk 1:7-8 | Lk 3:1-18

Strategic Context

John's call for repentance was not mere moral reform. It was a declaration that God's judgment was imminent. His message carried echoes of Isaiah, Malachi, and the Essenes, warning that God was about to intervene in history. By baptizing people in the Jordan, he symbolically reenacted Israel's entrance into the Promised Land, preparing them for another divine conquest—this time against Sin, Death, Chaos and the corrupt power of this world's leaders.

John's preaching, with its apocalyptic overtones, mirrored that of other end-time movements in Jewish history, particularly the Essenes at Qumran, who also awaited divine intervention and purification of Israel. His emphasis on baptism and wilderness withdrawal aligned with this mysterious wilderness group.

As a legitimate political threat due to the fervor it had stirred among the Jewish people, John's movement was a direct challenge to both Rome and the Jewish elite. By baptizing Jews, he suggested that the Temple-based sacrificial system was insufficient for true purification. His call for radical repentance undermined the authority of the priesthood and Pharisees. And his growing influence led Herod Antipas to see him as a potential revolutionary—and rightly so.

Geographical Insight

John deliberately operated in the Judean Wilderness, outside the reach of Rome and the central powers. The Judean wilderness was the setting for previous prophetic encounters and divine interventions, including Moses and Elijah, and even the famous Maccabees.

Baptism in the Jordan River was not just a ritual. It was an echo of Joshua's conquest of Canaan. John's movement signified a new beginning, a preparation for the ultimate battle against Sin, Death, and Chaos, and against corrupt human establishments of all kinds.

Tactical Insight

John was a Forerunner, and his mission was not just preparation in a spiritual sense. It was also designed to prepare the Jewish people in a revolutionary sense of softening enemy defenses by gathering a base of committed followers before the true revolution began with Jesus.

Baptism was a symbol of defiance. While purification rituals were common, John's public, large-scale initiatory, baptismal movement circumvented the Temple system, creating a new mode of initiation outside priestly control. Baptism was a public mark of allegiance to the Empire of God, inaugurated by John and fulfilled in Jesus.

Political Fallout

Herod Antipas quickly grew suspicious of John. John's movement grew too large to ignore. He was arrested (and later executed), not just for theological reasons, but because he was a social and political threat—a man who could incite rebellion against the status quo. His fate foreshadowed Jesus' own confrontation with the authorities.

Strategic Questions

1. Why the wilderness? John likely saw the desert as a place of purification and divine encounter, but it also kept his movement beyond the immediate control of Roman and Jewish authorities.

2. Why baptize in the Jordan? The Jordan symbolized entry into the Promised Land and divine renewal, making it the perfect setting for a movement that claimed God was about to restore His rule.

3. Why did John challenge Herod Antipas? John viewed Herod as a corrupt and illegitimate ruler. And in line with prophetic tradition, he called him to account, knowing full well the consequences.

4. What role did John play in Jesus' movement? John's movement laid the foundation for Jesus' own insurgency, gathering followers, preparing disciples, attracting attention, and setting the stage for the final confrontation with the powers of the world.

—SCENE 4—
THE RALLYING CRY

Jesus' Insurrection Inaugurated | Bethany, East of the Jordan River | Early 27 AD

Campaign Chronology

- **Jesus' Baptism |** Mt 3:13-17 | Mk 1:9-11 | Lk 3:21-23
- **Jesus' Temptation in the Desert |** Mt 4:1-11 | Mk 1:12-13 | Lk 4:1-13
- **John's Testimony about Himself |** Jn 1:19-28
- **John's Declaration to Jesus |** Jn 1:29-34

Geographical Insight

Bethany beyond the Jordan, east of the Jordan River, was outside Herod Antipas' jurisdiction, making it a relatively safe zone for both John and Jesus to operate without immediate interference from the authorities. It also connected symbolically to Elijah's ascension, reinforcing John's role as Elijah's prophetic successor (Malachi 4:5).

The Jordan River was filled with historic symbolism. Crossing the Jordan wasn't just a geographical move. It was a prophetic act. Just as Joshua led Israel into the Promised Land, Jesus was initiating a new Exodus, leading his people into a new Kingdom. His baptism in these waters signified not only a personal anointing but also the dawn of a nationwide uprising against the kingdom of darkness and its earthly agents.

Tactical Insight

Baptism was a public oath. In ancient Near Eastern, Roman, Jewish cultures, water rituals were often rites of passage. Baptism in John's movement wasn't just about personal repentance. It was an oath of allegiance to the coming Empire of God. Jesus, by undergoing this ritual, was publicly declaring himself part of a divine revolution.

The descent of the Holy Spirit like a dove was not just a private spiritual experience. It was a royal anointing, paralleling the coronation of Israel's kings. Jesus' baptism functioned as his official, public commissioning to begin the campaign.

Jesus' forty-day trial in the wilderness mirrored Israel's forty-year test in the wilderness and Moses' own forty-day fast on Sinai (Exodus 34:28). This was a strategic withdrawal—not one of weakness, but one of preparation before war. In the desert, Jesus confronted and defeated Satan, showing that his Empire would be built not through compromise or earthly power, but through divine authority and endurance.

Political Insight

In what was perceived as a challenge to Roman and Jewish authorities, Jesus' baptism by John placed him in a movement already under scrutiny. Rome and the Temple elite already saw John's movement as a threat because it functioned outside the Temple system. Jesus aligning himself with John made him an immediate target.

Jesus' withdrawal into the desert signaled that his Empire was not aligned with earthly power structures. Unlike Rome, which built its empire through military conquest, Jesus' Empire of Heaven would advance through love, transformation, and subversive acts of faith.

Strategic Questions

1. Why withdraw after baptism? Rather than immediately engaging in public ministry, Jesus retreated to solidify his strategy and test his own resolve. This ensured that when he emerged, he was fully prepared for the battles ahead.

2. Why was Jesus baptized if he was sinless? Jesus wasn't baptized for personal repentance but as an act of solidarity with the movement he came to launch and the people he came to save. He was publicly aligning himself with the revolutionary movement John had started, showing that he stood with the oppressed and the outcasts.

3. Why did Satan tempt Jesus with power? Satan offered Jesus the kingdoms of the world—a shortcut to dominion without the cross. Jesus refused, demonstrating that his rule would come not through violent acts or earthly politics—whether good or not—but through divine surrender to and victory over Death itself.

4. Why was baptism essential for Jesus' mission? It wasn't just about symbolism—it was the formal declaration that his campaign had begun. It was his public enlistment into the war against Sin, Death, Chaos, hatred, division, and corruption, showing that his heavenly Empire was already breaking into history.

—SCENE 5—
THE FIRST STRIKE

Firsts | Bethany, Cana, Capernaum, Jerusalem, Aenon near Salim | Early–Spring 27 AD

Campaign Chronology

- **First Encounters with Disciples |** Jn 1:35-51
- **Formal Calling of First Four Disciples |** Mt 4:18-22 | Mk 1:16-20 | Lk 5:1-11
- **Jesus' First Miracle |** Jn 2:1-11
- **Jesus' First Stay in Capernaum |** Jn 2:12
- **First Strike on the Temple—Passover 1 |** Jn 2:13-22
- **Early Responses to Jesus' Miracles |** Jn 2:23-25
- **Jesus' Encounter with Nicodemus |** Jn 3:1-21
- **Jesus' Wilderness Retreat, Meeting with John |** Jn 3:22-30
  - o **Jesus and John Baptize Others |** Jn 3:22, 26
  - o **Jesus Meets with John |** Jn 3:22-24
  - o **Jesus Gaining Followers from John |** Jn 3:25-26
  - o **John's Response |** Jn 3:27-30

Social, Religious & Political Context

Jesus' miracles and radical teachings quickly drew crowds, making him a figure of growing influence and gaining him early popularity in Galilee. This rising popularity raised alarms among Jewish leaders and

Roman authorities, who saw any grassroots movement as a potential threat to stability, especially in a region known for revolts.

The Jerusalem Temple complex was the beating heart of Jewish life—socially, religiously, economically, and politically. The priestly elite, particularly the Sadducees, wielded immense power over Temple operations, including financial transactions that funded both the institution and their own wealth.

Tactical Insight

Jesus' first miracle—transformation of water into wine at a wedding—which took place at Cana in Galilee, was more than a mere act of hospitality. It was a symbol of divine generosity, overturning scarcity with abundance. In a world ruled by economic exploitation, this miracle hinted at the radical provision of Jesus' new Empire, where the last would be first and the kingdom's resources would not be hoarded by the elite.

Jesus' strike against the Temple at Passover 1 was his first major confrontation with the Temple elite. It was not merely about money changers but about the systemic corruption that prevented genuine worshippers from encountering God. The marketplace had overtaken the outer courts—the space designated for Gentiles and seekers to draw near to God. Instead of providing access, the ruling class had monetized divine encounter, creating barriers where all should have been welcomed openly.

The strategic timing of Jesus' first visit to Jerusalem occurred before he had widespread notoriety. Unlike his later, highly anticipated entry into the city, this first strike was more of a reconnaissance mission—a test of the opposition's response. By purging the Temple at this early stage, he set a precedent: his movement was not just about moral reform, but about restructuring the very foundations of society. He was also unknown in Jerusalem at this early stage. With tens of thousands of worshippers in Jerusalem and the Temple precinct, an unknown man causing a stir in one segment of the Temple would have drawn some response from security forces, but not enough to sabotage his campaign, and fleeing without being identified or caught would have been relatively easy at this point. The situation would be different the next time around.

Strategic Questions

1. Why challenge the Temple system so early? Jesus knew that the Temple was the epicenter of Jewish life—social, economic, religious, and political. By striking at its corruption, he was not just making a

moral statement but signaling that his Empire would replace the old system entirely.

2. Why was he able to get away with it? At this stage, few in Jerusalem knew who Jesus was. He could strike the establishment, withdraw, and regroup before the authorities had time to organize against him. This was a tactical maneuver—a stick and move, a strike and retreat—giving him time to build his movement.

3. What did this foreshadow? The second Temple cleansing, which would come later in his campaign, would be far riskier. By then, Jesus was a well-known figure, and his return to the Temple would be an act of open defiance, forcing the authorities to act decisively.

4. Was this just about money changers? No. This was an attack on the entire system of power that had entrenched itself in the Temple— one that excluded the poor, oppressed the people, and served the interests of the wealthy and powerful elite rather than God. This was not just a religious protest. It was a declaration of war.

—SCENE 6—
THE INFILTRATION

Jesus' Departure from Judea & Return to Galilee | Judea, Samaria, Galilee | Spring–Fall 27 AD

Campaign Chronology

- **Departure from Judea** | Jn 4:1-4
- **Rebuke of Herod** | Lk 3:19-20
- **Return to Galilee** | Mt 4:12 | Mk 1:14 | Lk 4:14
- **Jesus & the Samaritan Woman** | Jn 4:5-38
- **Stay in Sychar** | Jn 4:39-42
- **Arrival in Galilee** | Jn 4:43-45

Geographical Insight

Most Jews avoided Samaria, viewing Samaritans as religiously impure and politically suspect. The long-standing hostility between Jews and Samaritans traced back to the Assyrian exile and the differing interpretations of the Torah. By traveling through Samaria instead of bypassing it, Jesus not only rejected these cultural divisions but also made a bold statement that his Empire was for all, not just the religious elite of Judea or Galilee.

Tactical Insight

Engaging in conversation with a Samaritan woman, particularly one with a questionable reputation, defied every social boundary of the time. This was not a casual interaction. It was a direct challenge to exclusionary social customs and religious practices that were deeply rooted in Jesus' culture. His offer of "living water" subverted traditional temple-based worship, emphasizing that true communion with God would no longer be tied to sacred geography but to the presence of God himself.

A viral message among the outcasts, the woman's transformation into a messenger for Jesus within her own community was a tactical move. Rather than trying to convince the religious elite, Jesus empowered those whom society had discarded, turning them into his first heralds in enemy territory. The Samaritan woman became an unlikely but effective evangelist, spreading Jesus' message where Jewish leaders could not intervene.

In attempt to avoid premature arrest, Jesus did not linger in Jerusalem after the Passover confrontations. Instead, he retreated northward to Galilee, where his growing movement could operate with more flexibility. Avoiding prolonged exposure in the capital allowed him to refine his strategy, train his disciples, and build a broader support base before facing the inevitable confrontation with the authorities—and ultimately, with Death.

Strategic Question

1. Why operate in the margins first? Jesus' mission was not aimed at the political and religious elite but at the disempowered, the overlooked, and the oppressed. By first building a grassroots movement among the disenfranchised, he created a decentralized, harder-to-control network of followers.

2. What did engaging with Samaritans accomplish? It demonstrated that his Empire was not bound by ethnic or religious borders. By prioritizing the Samaritans—who were despised by the Jewish establishment—Jesus signaled that his kingdom would upend the existing order, elevating those whom the religious authorities had written off.

3. Why was avoiding Jerusalem at this stage critical? The capital city—with the capitol building, the Temple, at its heart—was the stronghold of both the Jewish elite and Roman power. Remaining there too long would have escalated opposition too quickly, cutting short his mission before his movement was fully established. By

returning to Galilee, Jesus ensured that his insurgency would continue gathering strength before its final confrontation.

4. How does this challenge the existing power structures? By reaching out to Samaritans, women, and "sinners," Jesus undermined the societal and religious gatekeeping of the Temple authorities. He refused to let them dictate who had access to God, dismantling the barriers they had carefully constructed over generations. His revolution was not just against Rome. It was against any system that sought to control or regulate access to the divine presence.

The Revolt Intensifies

The revolution was no longer a whisper in the wilderness. It had become an open movement spreading across Galilee and beyond. Jesus shifted from mobilization to full-scale engagement. His choice of Capernaum as headquarters was no accident. It sat on a major trade route, ensuring his message reached Jews, Gentiles, and even Roman officials. He was not merely gathering followers, but he was recruiting soldiers for an Empire that defied both Rome and the religious elite.

This phase saw Jesus escalate his confrontation with the establishment. By calling a tax collector as a disciple, dining with sinners, and breaking Sabbath traditions, he openly challenged the economic, social, and religious power structures of the time. His growing defiance reached a climax during Passover in Jerusalem, where he had struck at the heart of the Temple system, declaring himself not only a teacher but a ruler with divine authority.

But the Empire of Heaven was not a mere earthly uprising. It was an assault against the very forces of Sin, Death, and Chaos. Through his miracles, Jesus asserted his power over disease, nature, and the demonic realm, signaling that his war was being waged on two fronts: the visible and the unseen. The storm was rising. The opposition was growing. And as the movement expanded, so did the danger. Jerusalem loomed on the horizon, but Jesus was not yet ready for the final battle. First, he needed to prepare his disciples and test their loyalty. The time for subtlety was over. The Empire was advancing.

—SCENE 7—
THE ADVANCE

Jesus' New Headquarters in Capernaum, Galilee | Galilee | Fall–Winter 27 AD

Campaign Chronology

- **The Empire of God is Near** | Mt 4:17 | Mk 1:14-15 | Lk 4:14-15
- **Boy Healed in Capernaum from Cana** | Jn 4:46-54
- **Declaration, Rejection at Nazareth** | Lk 4:16-31
- **Move to Capernaum** | Mt 4:13-16

Climate & Seasonal Context

Fall in Galilee was the perfect time for a public campaign to expand. With the harvest season in full swing, Galilean markets and roads were bustling with trade, drawing people from across the region. The Sea of Galilee served as a major artery of commerce and travel, ensuring that news of Jesus' activities would spread rapidly. And the cooler autumn temperatures made prolonged outdoor gatherings and public teaching much easier than in the peak heat of summer.

Geographical Insight

Capernaum became Jesus' base of operations. His decision to establish his headquarters in Capernaum was not arbitrary. This was a thriving border town between the territories of Herod Antipas and Herod Philip, meaning it was a political and commercial crossroads. This gave Jesus access to a wide array of people—Jewish locals, Roman officials, tax collectors, fishermen, and travelers passing through.

- Via Maris ("Way of the Sea"): Capernaum sat on this major trade route, connecting Egypt to Damascus, allowing his message to spread beyond Galilee.
- Roman Garrison Presence: The town housed a centurion, tax collection offices, and Roman patrols, making it an important administrative post.
- Jewish Leadership: Though heavily influenced by Rome, Capernaum also had a strong Jewish identity, with a synagogue that would become a central battleground for Jesus' teachings.

Tactical Insight

Jesus knew how to make strategic alliances using social customs. Capernaum was not just a place of miracles. It was a place where Jesus made key connections, including with powerful Roman and Jewish figures. His healing of a Roman centurion's servant (Matthew 8:5–13, Luke 7:1–10) was particularly significant.

Honor-Shame social dynamics were deeply at play in every public interaction Jesus had. The centurion, a Roman officer, publicly expressed faith in Jesus. By acknowledging Jesus' authority, he placed himself in a position of reciprocal obligation. That is, because Jesus helped the centurion, the centurion owed Jesus a favor back—and was now publicly "on the hook" by witnesses—in return for Jesus' healing of his son.

Due to the Roman officer's social standing and political power, this act would have gained Jesus a measure of social clout, as the centurion's endorsement would have made local authorities hesitant to move against Jesus too quickly. After all, if even a Roman officer respected Jesus, silencing him would not be simple.

Local Jewish leaders were already entangled in Roman politics, and this miracle further complicated things. Some of these leaders may have felt compelled to tolerate Jesus rather than directly oppose him, given that Jesus had gained some level of security from the local Roman forces.

By calling outsiders to join his movement, Jesus was building a coalition of the marginalized. Capernaum was also where Jesus called Matthew (Levi), the tax collector (Matthew 9:9). This was a deeply symbolic move. Tax collectors were seen as traitors to the Jewish people due to their collaboration with Rome, yet Jesus welcomed them into his movement. By doing so, he undermined the religious elite's authority, brought in figures with deep knowledge of economic systems, and signaled that his Empire would be built from the outcasts inward, not from the socially or religiously privileged outward.

Strategic Questions

1. Why did Jesus choose Capernaum instead of returning to Nazareth? Nazareth was a small, insular town with little political or economic influence. Its rejection of Jesus (Luke 4:24) showed that it was not fertile ground for his movement. Capernaum, by contrast, was a trade hub where his message could spread quickly and where he could interact with key figures who could either become allies or be forced into submission by social dynamics.

2. How did Jesus' miracles here serve as more than just acts of compassion? Each miracle was also a strategic move to shift the balance of power. Healing the centurion's servant flipped the Roman honor system, calling a tax collector forced local elites to react, and curing the sick in public built momentum and credibility for his movement.

3. Did Jesus gain protection by operating in Capernaum? While not full immunity, his connections with the centurion and other influential figures discouraged suppression by Jewish leaders. Roman authorities tended to avoid unnecessary disruptions in cooperative regions—if a centurion admired Jesus, local rulers would have preferred to watch and wait rather than move against him too soon.

4. How did Capernaum set the stage for the larger conflict? Jesus' actions in Capernaum were not just about spreading his message—they were about recruiting, testing the waters, and exposing the

fractures in Jewish-Roman relations. He gained both followers and enemies, setting the stage for his escalating confrontation with both Jewish leadership and imperial forces.

Calling of Matthew, Healings & Controversy | Galilee | Winter 27–Spring 28 AD

Campaign Chronology

- **Teaching, Healing in Capernaum** | Mk 1:21-28 | Lk 4:31-37
- **Peter's Mother-in-Law Healed** | Mt 8:14-17 | Mk 1:29-34 | Lk 4:38-41
- **Tour of Galilee with Simon, Others** | Mt 4:23-25 | Mk 1:35-39 | Lk 4:42-44
- **Cleansing of Man with Leprosy** | Mt 8:2-3 | Mk 1:40-42 | Lk 5:12-13
- **Publicity After Cleansing** | Mt 8:4 | Mk 1:43-45 | Lk 5:14-16
- **Forgiving, Healing of Paralytic** | Mt 9:1-8 | Mk 2:1-12 | Lk 5:17-26
- **Calling of Matthew/Levi** | Mt 9:9 | Mk 2:13-14 | Lk 5:27-28
- **Banquet at Matthew's House** | Mt 9:10-13 | Mk 2:15-17 | Lk 5:29-32
- **Defense of Disciples for not Fasting** | Mt 9:14-17 | Mk 2:18-22 | Lk 5:33-39

Climate & Seasonal Context

Winter in Galilee was a season of opportunity amidst hardship. Winter was mild compared to other regions, with temperatures averaging between 50–60°F. However, the rainy season made travel slow and difficult, turning dirt roads into mud and reducing access to open-air gatherings. The seasonal downturn in agriculture and fishing meant that common laborers had more free time, creating an opportune moment for Jesus to gather followers. While winter posed logistical challenges, it also allowed his message to reach a wider audience, particularly among those most affected by economic hardship.

Geographical Insight

Located on the Via Maris trade route, Capernaum was an economic hub where Roman oversight and Jewish religious life intersected. The presence of a tax station and a Roman garrison meant that both political and economic power were in constant tension with the daily lives of ordinary Jews. Jesus' decision to base much of his ministry here was no accident. It was the perfect location for an alliance with and a challenge to both the Roman and Jewish elites.

The tax system was notorious for enriching a few while burdening the majority. Tax collectors like Matthew were viewed as traitors, benefiting from Roman exploitation at the expense of their own people.

The town housed Roman officials, including a centurion, whose servant Jesus healed (Luke 7:1-10). This act of mercy toward an occupying force flipped the honor-shame dynamic, creating social debts that may have provided Jesus with a degree of local protection.

As a bustling, culturally diverse town with traders, soldiers, and religious teachers passing through, Capernaum was an ideal launching pad for a movement that aimed to spread beyond Galilee.

Tactical Insight

Jesus' recruitment of Matthew was more than just a display of grace. It was an intentional move to subvert the existing power structures. It was a direct challenge to economic oppression. By calling a tax collector into his movement, Jesus signaled that his Empire was open to even the most despised members of society. It was a declaration that the old system of wealth and privilege had no place in his kingdom. It also forced a public crisis. By eating with tax collectors and sinners, Jesus put religious leaders in an impossible position. Either they had to accept that God's mercy extended to outcasts, or they had to expose their own hypocrisy. Here, too, Jesus was able to leverage additional influence. Matthew's wealth and connections meant that Jesus' movement now had access to people on the fringes of both Jewish and Roman power.

Sabbath healings were deliberate acts of defiance. Jesus didn't just heal on the Sabbath. He healed publicly and provocatively, forcing confrontations with religious authorities. He did so by exposing legalism. When Jesus healed a man's withered hand in the synagogue on the Sabbath (Mark 3:1-6), it wasn't just an act of mercy—it was a calculated move to highlight the hypocrisy of those who valued rules over human life. He was also provoking his opponents. Every Sabbath healing escalated tensions, pushing religious leaders closer to open opposition. This was not a passive mission; Jesus was intentionally forcing them to reveal their priorities. And in healing on the Sabbath, Jesus was also redefining authority. By demonstrating that he, not the religious elite, had the authority to interpret God's will, Jesus positioned himself as the true leader of Israel.

Strategic Questions

1. Why recruit a tax collector? Calling Matthew was not just about redemption—it was a public statement against economic injustice. It also created a scandal that forced religious leaders to take a position on Jesus' movement.

2. Why provoke Sabbath controversies? Jesus was forcing religious leaders to show their true colors. If they opposed healing, they exposed themselves as valuing rules over people. If they allowed it, they ceded moral authority to Jesus. Either way, he was winning the ideological battle.

3. How did Capernaum shape Jesus' movement? Capernaum's mix of Jewish tradition, Roman oversight, and economic influence made it the perfect setting for challenging the establishment. Its trade connections ensured that Jesus' message would spread beyond Galilee.

4. How did Jesus' early actions build momentum for his campaign? By challenging both religious and political authorities, Jesus turned his movement into a revolutionary force. He wasn't just preaching—he was actively dismantling the structures of power, setting the stage for the coming storm.

—SCENE 9—
THE RISING STORM

Jesus' Insurrection Continued, Passover 2 | Jerusalem | Spring 28 AD

Campaign Chronology

- **Healing of Disabled on Sabbath |** Jn 5:1-9, 6:4
- **Attempt on Jesus' Life |** Jn 5:10-18
- **The Son's Equality with the Father |** Jn 5:19-47
- **Picking Grain on the Sabbath |** Mt 12:1-8 | Mk 2:23-28 | Lk 6:1-5

Climate & Seasonal Context

Spring in Jerusalem was the peak pilgrimage season. The second Passover of Jesus' public campaign brought tens of thousands of Jewish pilgrims to Jerusalem. The normally bustling city swelled with travelers preparing for the festival. Days were warm (~60–75°F), and nights were cool (~50°F), making open-air teaching in the Temple courts common. Messianic expectations were at a fever pitch. Many believed this was the time when God would send a deliverer to free Israel from oppression.

Geographical Insight

The Temple was the heart of power. More than a place of worship, it was the center of social, religious, economic, and political authority. The Sadducean priestly elite maintained control by cooperating with Rome, and they benefited and profited very nicely from it.

The Pool of Bethesda was a place of desperation. Known for its supposed healing properties, Bethesda was a gathering site for the sick and disabled. It became the setting for one of Jesus' most provocative healings (John 5:1-9).

Synagogues and public spaces were hubs of debate. Beyond the Temple, Jesus engaged in discussions in synagogues and public forums, where Pharisees and scribes tested his growing influence.

Tactical Insight

Healing on the Sabbath was a calculated defiance. Jesus' choice to heal a paralyzed man at Bethesda on the Sabbath (John 5:1-9) was deliberate. It was not just an act of compassion but a direct challenge to the Pharisees' rigid legalism. They saw it as a violation of Torah, but Jesus reframed the debate: Was the Sabbath about rules or restoration? His actions exposed the leaders' hypocrisy, asserting that his mission superseded their authority.

The outrage escalated when Jesus declared, "My Father is always at his work to this very day, and I too am working" (John 5:17). For many, in Jewish thought, calling God "Father" in such a personal way implied equality with God. Some of the leaders immediately sought to kill him (John 5:18). His claim made it clear: the old religious order was being replaced.

Jesus and his disciples plucked grain to eat on the Sabbath, angering the Pharisees (Matthew 12:1-8, Mark 2:23-28, Luke 6:1-5). He countered with the example of David eating consecrated bread (1 Samuel 21:1-6), exposing their hypocrisy. Then, he made an even bolder claim: "The Son of Man is Lord of the Sabbath" (Mark 2:28). This was revolutionary. The Sabbath was instituted by God, yet Jesus declared authority over it, signaling his rule over Israel itself.

Strategic Questions

1. Why did Jesus provoke conflict during Passover? The festival heightened Jewish hopes of deliverance. By challenging the religious elite at this key moment, he forced them to publicly oppose him, exposing their corruption.

2. Why was healing on the Sabbath so controversial? The Pharisees' power relied on their particular interpretation of the law.

Jesus shattered their system, showing that human suffering mattered more than any laws, and if one's interpretation caused another to suffer, then that interpretation was a violation of God's intent.

3. Why did Jesus declare himself "Lord of the Sabbath"? The Sabbath was a divine institution. By claiming lordship over it, Jesus made a claim to divinity—one his opponents saw as blasphemy.

4. How did these events shape the next phase of Jesus' mission? His confrontations in Jerusalem escalated the conflict, making it clear to the religious authorities that he was a threat. From this point, his path to the cross was set.

—SCENE 10—
THE CAMPAIGN GAINS MOMENTUM

Back to Galilee with the Crowds | Galilee | Spring 28 AD

Campaign Chronology

- **Healing the Man's Hand on Sabbath |** Mt 12:9-14 | Mk 3:1-6 | Lk 6:6-11
- **Withdrawal to Sea of Galilee |** Mt 12:15-21 | Mk 3:7-12
- **Commissioning of the Twelve Disciples |** Mt 10:1-4 | Mk 3:13-19 | Lk 6:12-16

Climate & Seasonal Context

Spring in Galilee brought mild temperatures and lush, green landscapes, making it an ideal time for large outdoor gatherings. The hills surrounding the Sea of Galilee created a natural amphitheater, allowing Jesus' voice to carry over great distances. The season also marked increased movement among rural populations, as farmers and fishermen had more freedom to travel and gather.

Geographical Insight

The Sea of Galilee was more than just a scenic backdrop. It was a strategic setting for Jesus' teaching. Its shores provided a space where large crowds could assemble without interference from local authorities. The region was also a major trade route, ensuring that his message would spread far beyond Galilee.

Capernaum remained Jesus' primary base, giving him access to both Jewish and Roman audiences. But his withdrawal from cities and synagogues into more open spaces signaled a shift in his tactics—his mission was not simply religious, but he was making it clear that it was social and political as well.

Tactical Insight

After escalating tensions in Jerusalem, Jesus withdrew to Galilee to regroup and refocus. This was not a retreat in the conventional sense but a strategic recalibration. By shifting his teaching from synagogues to open spaces near the sea, he reduced the risk of direct confrontation with religious authorities while amplifying his influence among the common people (*am ha-aretz*).

His decision to call twelve disciples was a direct statement of restoration. The number twelve mirrored the twelve tribes of Israel, signaling a renewed national identity under his leadership. This was not just about mentorship. It was an intentional move to establish a structured leadership core, a "messianic elite," preparing for the expansion of his movement.

Strategic Questions

1. Why withdraw to the sea rather than remain in synagogues? Moving to open spaces allowed Jesus to control the narrative, avoiding interruptions from hostile religious leaders while engaging directly with—and recruiting—the common people.

2. Why appoint exactly twelve disciples? The number was symbolic of Israel's restoration, positioning Jesus as the leader of a renewed people under God's rule.

3. How did this withdrawal serve his broader strategy? By pulling away from immediate threats in Jerusalem, Jesus was able to build a stronger base of followers in Galilee before making his next decisive move.

4. Why was this period such a crucial turning point in Jesus' campaign? While opposition from religious leaders was growing, so was his popular support. By retreating to Galilee, he strengthened his movement, trained his closest followers, and ensured that his message would continue spreading—even as the conflict with the authorities loomed ever closer.

—SCENE 11—
DECLARATION OF A REVOLUTION

Constitution of the New Empire | Mountainside, Sea of Galilee | Spring 28 AD

Campaign Chronology

- **Setting of the Imperial Constitution |** Mt 5:1-2 | Lk 6:17-19
- **Blessings & Curses |** Mt 5:3-12 | Lk 6:20-26

- **Salt & Light** | Mt 5:13-16
- **Law, Righteousness & the Empire** | Mt 5:17-20
- **Oral versus Jesus on the Law** | Mt 5:21-48 | Lk 6:27-36
- **Hypocritical Acts of Righteousness** | Mt 6:1-18
- **Greed, Eyes, Money, Worry** | Mt 6:19-7:6 | Lk 6:37-42
- **Ask, Enter, Listen, Golden Rule** | Mt 7:7-27 | Lk 6:31, 43-49
- **Crowds' Amazement at Jesus' Teaching** | Mt 7:28-8:1

Climate & Seasonal Context

With the dry season beginning in Galilee, crowds could gather freely without the constraints of rain or mud. This allowed for extended public assemblies, crucial for a movement seeking to establish a foothold among the people. The hills provided an ideal stage for mass communication—elevated and open-air, but also symbolic of past revolutionary moments in Israel's history and reminiscent of recent revolts among the Jews of Jesus' lifetime.

Geographical Insight

The hills of Galilee provided a natural amphitheater, allowing Jesus' message to carry across vast crowds. But more importantly, the setting invoked Sinai, where Moses delivered the Torah to Israel. By standing atop a mountain and delivering a manifesto, his Imperial Constitution, Jesus was positioning himself not just as a teacher, but as a new Moses—the establisher of a new nation and giver of a new Constitution—a revolutionary leader proclaiming the foundation of a new civilization.

Unlike Moses, however, Jesus was not merely offering laws to an already established nation. He was rallying the disenfranchised and organizing an insurrection. His message targeted the poor, the mourners, the persecuted—the very people most disillusioned by the ruling system of this world.

Tactical Insight

This was no ordinary "sermon." It was the Imperial Constitution of Jesus' alternative Empire. The so-called Beatitudes were a direct inversion of Rome's (and the world's) imperial values. In Rome, the powerful ruled by conquest. In Jesus' Empire, the meek would inherit. Rome's system favored the wealthy; Jesus blessed the poor. This was revolutionary rhetoric, a constitution for an insurrection against the prevailing social, religious, and political order.

Jesus did not offer vague religious encouragement. He redefined power itself. His "Blessings and Woes" stood in stark contrast to

Roman and Jewish elite structures, declaring that those society had rejected would be the ones to rule in the Empire he was establishing.

Jesus' reinterpretation of the Law went beyond the written Torah. He openly challenged the Pharisaic and Sadducean hold on religious life, reclaiming the Law's original intention. His contrast between "You have heard it said" and "But I say to you" was a deliberate act of seizing moral and legal authority from the establishment.

Jesus' warnings about wealth and hypocrisy attacked the financial and religious elite, exposing their system of oppression and calling for economic realignment. The Salt and Light imagery was a call to action. His followers were to be a revolutionary frontline, visibly embodying the radical and disruptive principles of his Empire.

Strategic Questions

1. How did this challenge Rome? The Beatitudes redefined power—favoring the meek over the mighty, the poor over the wealthy, the minorities over the majority, flipping the allegedly God-sanctioned social, religious, economic, and political order on its head.

2. Why present this message in public rather than in private among his disciples? This was not an esoteric teaching for an elite inner circle. It was a campaign rally, meant to be spread widely.

3. What was the risk of such a proclamation? This teaching was not just provocative. It was treasonous. To declare a new moral and social order, where the existing rulers were deposed and the outcasts exalted, was an open act of defiance against both Jewish leadership and Roman imperial control.

4. What made this the moment when Jesus' movement became unmistakably political? He was no longer a wandering teacher with vague spiritual ideals. He was a revolutionary commander, laying out the ideological framework of his Empire. The crowds marveled not just at his words, but at the authority with which he spoke. The Empire of God had been formally declared.

—SCENE 12—
SHOCKWAVES THROUGHOUT GALILEE

Growing Fame & Proclaiming Repentance | Galilee | Spring 28 AD

Campaign Chronology

- **Healing of Centurion's Servant |** Mt 8:5-13 | Lk 7:1-10
- **Raising of Widow's Son |** Lk 7:11-17
- **John the Baptist & the Empire |** Mt 11:2-19 | Lk 7:18-35
- **Woe to Korazin & Bethsaida |** Mt 11:20-30

- **Anointing of Jesus' Feet | Lk 7:36-50**

Climate & Seasonal Context

The dry season in Galilee brought intense heat, with temperatures ranging from 80–90°F. Travel was physically exhausting, yet the clear skies allowed for open-air gatherings where Jesus could teach large crowds. With no rain to interfere, the impact of his miracles—healings, feedings, and even raising the dead—became even more dramatic. The harsh conditions heightened the desperation of those seeking relief, making his ministry all the more compelling.

Geographical Insight

Jesus concentrated his ministry in three key towns—Capernaum, Nain, and Bethsaida—each playing a strategic role in his movement.

Capernaum, his home base, was a Roman administrative center with tax collectors, soldiers, and traders. Jesus had already gained influence here by interacting with both outcasts and officials.

Nain was a small, insignificant town that became the site of one of his most shocking miracles—rescuing a widow's son from Death.

Bethsaida was the hometown of several of his disciples, yet also a place of resistance, eventually earning Jesus' sharp rebuke.

Tactical Insight

This period was marked by a growing recognition of Jesus' power, escalating questions about his identity, and increasing opposition from both religious elites and everyday people.

Raising the widow's son in Nain echoed the stories of Elijah and Elisha, both of whom had raised the dead in times of national distress. By performing this act publicly, Jesus wasn't just comforting a grieving mother. He was making a bold declaration of divine authority. His ability to command life itself made him more than a healer. It positioned him as a direct challenger to the cosmic forces of Sin, Death and Chaos.

From prison, John the Baptist sent messengers asking, "Are you the one who is to come, or should we look for another?" (Luke 7:19). Instead of a direct answer, Jesus pointed to his actions—healing the sick, restoring sight to the blind, and proclaiming good news to the poor. This exchange revealed the tension between John's apocalyptic expectations of the Messiah and Jesus' mission of restoration rather than judgment. His response forced John's followers to discern the truth for themselves, demonstrating the required in Jesus' Empire.

While some towns welcomed Jesus, Bethsaida and Korazin refused to acknowledge his works. Jesus compared them to Tyre and Sidon—infamous cities condemned by the prophets—warning that their rejection would lead to judgment. This marked a turning point: Jesus was not seeking mere popularity. His Empire was for those willing to accept it, and refusal had consequences.

Strategic Questions

1. Why emphasize raising the dead? Since the beginning of human history, Death had ruled as the ultimate enemy—an unstoppable force that no king or warrior could defeat. In the ancient world, Death was more than a natural event. It was a power that enslaved humanity. Jesus' resurrections, like the widow's son in Nain (Luke 7:11-17) and Jairus' daughter (Mark 5:35-43), were more than acts of compassion. They were an assault on the very forces of Sin and Death. Unlike Elijah and Elisha, who called on God to raise the dead, Jesus commanded life by his own authority. Each resurrection foreshadowed his ultimate victory over Death at the empty tomb.

2. Why allow John the Baptist to doubt? John had boldly declared Jesus as the Messiah, but from prison, he began to question. He sent his followers to ask, "Are you the one who is to come, or should we look for another?" (Luke 7:19). Instead of a direct answer, Jesus pointed to the signs—the blind seeing, the disabled walking, and the good news preached to the poor. He left John to interpret the evidence. This was a lesson in faith—not blind belief, but the ability to recognize the Empire of God breaking into the world. The Kingdom would not be built by those waiting for easy answers, but by those willing to see and act.

3. Why rebuke entire cities like Bethsaida and Korazin? Despite witnessing miracles, Bethsaida and Korazin refused to acknowledge Jesus. He compared them unfavorably to Tyre and Sidon (Luke 10:13-15), cities known for their wickedness. This was not about doubt but deliberate rejection. Jesus' movement demanded commitment, not casual allegiance. By turning away, these cities chose to remain in a decaying order that would soon be overthrown.

4. Why had Jesus' campaign shifted from proclamation to reckoning? At first, Jesus preached, healed, and gathered followers. Now, everything escalated. His miracles became declarations of power. His teachings became challenges. His warnings became imminent threats. The time for choosing had arrived. Neutrality was no longer an option. The battle for allegiance had begun.

Galilee with Twelve, Growing Opposition | Galilee, Around the Sea | Spring–Summer 28 AD

Campaign Chronology

- **Tour with the Twelve & Others** | Lk 8:1-3
- **Accusations of Blasphemy** | Mt 12:22-37 | Mk 3:20-30
- **Refusal to Give a Miraculous Sign** | Mt 12:38-45
- **Announcement of New Kinship** | Mt 12:46-50 | Mk 3:31-35 | Lk 8:19-21
- **Empire in Parables around the Sea** | Mt 13:1-3 | Mk 4:1-2 | Lk 8:4
- *Parables to the Crowds* | Mt 13:3-35 | Mk 4:3-34 | Lk 8:5-18
  - **Parable of the Soils** | Mt 13:3-23 | Mk 4:3-25 | Lk 8:5-18
  - **Parable of the Seed's Growth** | Mk 4:26-29
  - **Parable of the Weeds** | Mt 13:24-30
  - **Parable of the Mustard Seed** | Mt 13:31-32 | Mk 4:30-32
  - **Parable of the Unleavened Bread** | Mt 13:33-35 | Mk 4:33-34
- *Parables to the Twelve* | Mt 13:36-53
  - **Parable of the Weeds Explained** | Mt 13:36-43
  - **Parable of the Hidden Treasure** | Mt 13:44
  - **Parable of the Pearl** | Mt 13:45-46
  - **Parable of the Net** | Mt 13:47-50
  - **Parable of the House Owner** | Mt 13:51-53
- **Defeat of the Sea Storm** | Mt 8:18, 23-27 | Mk 4:35-41 | Lk 8:22-25
- **Liberation of Demon-possessed in Gerasa** | Mt 8:28-34 | Mk 5:1-20 | Lk 8:26-39
- **Healing of Woman via Tzitzit** | Mt 9:18-26 | Mk 5:21-43 | Lk 8:40-56
- **Raising of Jairus' Daughter** | Mt 9:18-26 | Mk 5:21-43 | Lk 8:40-56
- **Battles against Sickness, Demons** | Mt 9:27-34
- **Final Visit to Nazareth** | Mt 13:54-58 | Mk 6:1-6

Climate & Seasonal Context

The dry season in Galilee brought intense heat, with temperatures soaring between 80–90°F. Travel was easier without the hindrance of rain, but the relentless sun made journeys exhausting. With the Sea of Galilee at the heart of his ministry, Jesus often preached by the water, where the cool breezes provided some relief. The long daylight hours allowed for extended teaching sessions, large public gatherings, and an increase in movement across the region.

Social, Religious & Political Context

By now, Jesus' movement was no longer operating in obscurity. His teachings, miracles, and growing base of followers had made him a target for the leaders. The Pharisees and scribes had begun publicly challenging him, questioning his authority and demanding signs to prove his legitimacy. Their opposition was not just theological—it was political. Jesus was redefining power, purity, and kinship, threatening the entire structure they upheld.

Meanwhile, Jesus was building his inner circle. The Twelve disciples were not just students. They were his appointed leaders, the ones who would spread his message and carry on his mission. But as opposition mounted, he shifted his teaching strategy, relying more heavily on parables—stories that concealed as much as they revealed, forcing his audience to wrestle with the meaning of his Empire.

Tactical Insight

Teaching in parables was more than just a clever way to make a religious point. It was a politically strategic move. With enemies watching his every word, Jesus adjusted his method. Parables became his way of speaking truth while hiding it from those who sought to twist his message. His stories about seeds, treasure, and a fishing net were not moral lessons. They were veiled declarations about his Empire. Those who had "ears to hear" would understand. Those who didn't were already rejecting him.

When told his mother and brothers were looking for him, Jesus responded, "Whoever does the will of my Father is my brother and sister and mother" (Matthew 12:50). This was not just a spiritual statement. It was a radical declaration that loyalty to God's Empire came before family ties, religious tradition, and national identity. He was forming a new kind of kinship, one based on allegiance to his rule.

Jesus engaged in an epic, two-part battle with the primal foe, Chaos—part one of which came in a boat ride across the Sea of Galilee. One night, as a violent storm overtook the Sea of Galilee, Jesus remained asleep in the boat. His disciples, panicked and terrified, woke him. At his command, the storm ceased instantly. In ancient Near Eastern, Israelite, and Jewish thought, the Sea was not just water—it was a symbol of Chaos, the great enemy of divine order, the incarnation of deities of disorder. This moment was not just about calming waves. It was an act of cosmic warfare. In the Bible, Yahweh subdued the primordial waters in creation (Genesis 1:2); he split the Red Sea to rescue Israel (Exodus 14); he rebuked the waters, forcing them into submission (Psalm 104:7). Jesus did the same. But instead of recognizing his power, the disciples only asked, "Who is this, that even the wind and Sea obey him?" (Mark 4:41). The battle against Chaos had begun, but they still didn't understand. Round two in the battle would need to wait until later.

In expanding his mission by breaking boundaries, Jesus' healing of the demon-possessed Gerasene (Mark 5:1-20) took place in Gentile territory, marking a turning point. This was not just a healing but an invasion into enemy ground. The demon's name, "Legion," echoed Roman military forces, reinforcing the idea that Jesus' power was both spiritual and political. The demons were cast into pigs and returned to their home—the depths of the Sea, the home of Death and Chaos. But rather than celebrate, the locals begged Jesus to leave. His power was too disruptive, too terrifying, and it cost them too much.

Raising the dead was a declaration of war on Death itself. Jesus healed the woman with the issue of blood and raised Jairus' daughter from the dead (Mark 5:21-43). Both acts were about more than just compassion. The woman had been ritually unclean for twelve years—an outcast. Jesus restored not only her health but her place in society. Jairus' daughter's resurrection was a foreshadowing of his greatest act—his eventual victory over Death itself.

Strategic Questions

1. Why switch to parables? As opposition from religious leaders intensified, Jesus shifted his teaching strategy. Parables allowed him to communicate deep truths while concealing them from those who would use his words against him (Matthew 13:10-17). To the crowds, these stories seemed like simple agricultural or household analogies, but to those with eyes to see, they contained the blueprint for his Empire. The parables weren't just moral. They were tactical—they separated those who truly sought the truth from those who were only looking to entrap him. This shift marked a crucial stage in his campaign. No longer speaking plainly to all, Jesus ensured that only those truly committed would understand the full scope of his mission.

2. Why redefine family? In a culture where family ties were everything, Jesus' statement, "Whoever does the will of my Father is my brother, sister, and mother" (Matthew 12:50), was radical. He was not just encouraging spiritual closeness. He was redefining the very concept of belonging. His Empire would not be built on ethnic lineage,

political loyalty, social status, or religious ties, but on allegiance to God. This wasn't just a metaphor but a political restructuring. The existing religious elite claimed authority through ancestry and law, but Jesus was forming a new kind of Israel, one where faithfulness, not birthright, determined one's place. His movement was a nation in the making, one that would soon stand in direct opposition to the religious and imperial powers of his time.

3. Why rebuke the Sea? Jesus' so-called calming of the storm (Matthew 8:18, 23-27, Mark 4:35-41, Luke 8:22-25) was not just an impressive display of power over nature—it was an act of divine warfare. In the ancient Near East and Hebrew Bible, the Sea was not merely water. It was Chaos, the primal force that stood against divine order. Yahweh's victories over the sea in Genesis 1, Exodus 14, Psalm 74, and Isaiah 51 were not just moments of control—they were acts of conquest. The Sea was the realm of the deep, the dwelling place of Leviathan (Israel), the incarnation of Tiamat (Mesopotamia) or Yamm (Canaan)—the ferocious dragonlike deity of disorder. Jesus, asleep in the boat, fit an ancient pattern—the sleeping king or god who rises to battle Chaos. In Psalm 44:23, Israel cries, "Awake, Lord! Why do you sleep?" Jesus' disciples, terrified by the storm, echoed this when they woke him in panic. And like Yahweh, who rebuked the Sea in the Old Testament, Jesus rebuked the wind and waves. And they obeyed. This was a direct assertion of divine authority. The disciples, however, did not yet grasp what had just happened. Instead of praising him, they were struck with awe and fear: "Who then is this, that even the wind and the Sea obey him?" (Mark 4:41). They did not yet see that they were standing in the presence of the Son of God, the one who ruled over the great enemy, Chaos itself. But they would soon understand in part two of this war against the sea (Matthew 14), when Jesus would walk upon the waves to prove his dominion fully.

4. Why did the people of Gerasa reject Jesus? Jesus' exorcism of the Gerasene demon-possessed (Mark 5:1-20) was not just an act of healing. It was an assault on a demonic stronghold. The demons called themselves Legion—a term loaded with Roman military significance, suggesting not just spiritual oppression, but political overtones of occupation and control. By casting them into a herd of pigs, Jesus demonstrated total dominion over them, sending them back into the depths, the place of Chaos. But the people of the region did not respond with gratitude. Instead, they begged Jesus to leave. Why? Because his power had real-world consequences. The destruction of the pigs was an economic catastrophe. Their livelihood was gone, and they were faced with a choice: embrace Jesus and his new order, or

cling to the security of what they had always known. They chose economic comfort over divine transformation.

5. What was it about this phase of Jesus' campaign that exposed fault lines? Up to this point, Jesus had been gaining followers, performing miracles, and teaching about the Empire of God. But now, his campaign was forcing people to make a choice. His parables were no longer just wisdom. They were veiled challenges. And his miracles weren't just acts of compassion. They were declarations of divine rule. His rebuke of the Sea, his redefinition of family, and his confrontations with both spiritual and earthly authorities were escalating the conflict. Some embraced his message. Others recoiled. The question was no longer if a final confrontation was coming—but when.

Shoring Up Regional Support

With growing momentum behind him, Jesus launched a final, coordinated offensive in Galilee. No longer a scattered movement, his empire-building efforts became more structured, with his disciples deployed in pairs to spread the message. This mirrored ancient military scouting tactics—securing regional footholds while avoiding immediate confrontation with Rome. Yet, Jesus' challenge to both the religious and political elite intensified.

John the Baptist, whose campaign once paved the way for Jesus, was executed by Herod Antipas—a clear warning that revolutionary figures would not be tolerated. This signaled a shift: Jesus' mission would no longer operate in the relative safety of Galilee for much longer. His next moves—feeding multitudes in a wilderness setting, walking on water as a demonstration of divine authority over Chaos, and delivering his controversial "Bread of Life" discourse—thinned the ranks of his followers. Many abandoned him, as he knew would happen, when he refused to be a conventional messianic leader.

Retreating to Gentile regions like Tyre and Sidon, Jesus tested his disciples' faith and refined his inner circle. At Caesarea Philippi, Peter finally declared Jesus as the Messiah. The Transfiguration, high on a mountain, cemented Jesus' identity and prepared his followers for the final campaign: the march on Jerusalem.

—SCENE 14—
THE COMMISSION & THE FALLEN PROPHET

Commission of Twelve, Beheading of John| Galilee, Near the Sea, Ituraea | Summer 28 AD

Campaign Chronology

- **Synagogue Campaign** | Mt 9:35-38 | Mk 6:6
- **Commissioning of Disciples in Pairs** | Mt 10:1-42 | Mk 6:7-11 | Lk 9:1-5
- **Disciples Sent** | Mt 11:1 | Mk 6:12-13 | Lk 9:6
- **Herod Antipas & Jesus** | Mt 14:1-2 | Mk 6:14-16 | Lk 9:7-9
- **John's Imprisonment, Beheading** | Mt 14:3-12 | Mk 6:17-29
- **Return of Disciples** | Mk 6:30 | Lk 9:10

Social, Religious & Political Context

The Jesus movement was reaching a critical juncture. Until now, Jesus had been gathering followers, gaining influence, and subtly challenging the religious and political authorities. But two events marked a dramatic escalation—the beheading of John the Baptist and the commissioning of the Twelve. John's execution at the hands of Herod Antipas sent a clear warning: messianic figures and their movements were being watched. His death was not just personal—it was strategic. Removing John was an attempt to decapitate the movement before it could spread further. Meanwhile, Jesus intensified his own offensive strategy, commissioning his closest disciples and deploying them in pairs. It also multiplied his influence, as his followers became heralds of the Empire, signaling an expansion of the movement.

Tactical Insight

The commissioning of the Twelve was a tactical deployment. In doing so, Jesus was shifting his strategy—instead of working alone, he deployed disciples in pairs, creating a network of influence across Galilee. This mimicked military scouting tactics, where operatives moved ahead of the leader, gathering intelligence, securing alliances, and preparing the ground for larger movements. The Twelve were not just preachers—they were insurgents in a cultural and religious revolution. They healed, cast out demons, and announced the arrival of the Empire.

Pairs provided strength, protection, and credibility. Sending two disciples per mission ensured they could verify each other's words, avoiding accusations of fraud (Deuteronomy 19:15). In a hostile environment, two travelers were safer than one, reinforcing their resilience against opposition. Working in pairs allowed one to speak while the other observed, improving adaptability and strategy.

John the Baptist's beheading was a warning message from the authorities. John's execution was a turning point. Jesus' movement was no longer operating in relative safety. Herod Antipas' paranoia had been growing, as John had openly criticized his unlawful marriage (Mark 6:17-18), making him a political nuisance as well as a religious one. But the real threat? John had become a rallying figure, his influence extending beyond religious boundaries into social and political resistance against oppression and corruption.

Herod feared Jesus after John's death. John's beheading was supposed to quell the rebellion, yet Jesus' movement only grew stronger. Herod heard rumors that Jesus might be John resurrected

(Matthew 14:1-2). This wasn't just superstition. It reflected the authorities' growing fear that Jesus was continuing John's mission, but with even greater influence.

After their missions, the disciples returned with more strength and more tested for battle. They returned with greater confidence, hardened by opposition. Their reports provided intelligence and fuel for the strategy and tactics Jesus would employ in the next phase of his messianic campaign. He now had proof that his movement could survive beyond his personal, physical presence.

Strategic Questions

1. Why did Jesus commission disciples now? With John eliminated, Jesus accelerated his mission, ensuring that his message would spread rapidly before authorities could shut him down.

2. What made John's death a turning point? His execution signaled that Rome and Herod were now actively suppressing messianic movements, increasing the urgency for Jesus to expand his operations.

3. Why was Herod so afraid of Jesus? Despite executing John, Herod could not kill the movement. And Jesus' growing influence suggested that the revolution was far from over.

4. Why did the disciples return stronger? Facing opposition firsthand toughened them, forcing them to rely on faith, strategy, and each other—a critical preparation for what lay ahead.

—SCENE 15—
THE SURGE & THE SIFTING

Feeding of the People & Defeat of the Sea | Galilee, Near the Sea, Ituraea | Summer 28 AD

Campaign Chronology

- **Retreat to Bethsaida near Julias** | Mt 14:13-14 | Mk 6:31-34 | Lk 9:10-11 | Jn 6:1-3
- **Feeding of Five Thousand** | Mt 14:15-21 | Mk 6:35-44 | Lk 9:12-17 | Jn 6:5-13
- **Attempt to Make Jesus King** | Mt 14:22-23 | Mk 6:45-46 | Jn 6:14-15
- **Walking on Water & (Divine) Sonship** | Mt 14:24-33 | Mk 6:47-52 | Jn 6:16-21
- **Healings at Gennesaret** | Mt 14:34-36 | Mk 6:53-56
- **Bread of Life Discourse at Capernaum** | Jn 6:22-59
- **Defection among Followers** | Jn 6:60-71

Climate & Seasonal Context

The Galilean summer was hot and dry, with temperatures often reaching 90°F (32°C). By this time of year, food scarcity was a growing concern, making Jesus' feeding of the five thousand even more remarkable. The crowds gathering around him were not just hungry for food but also for a leader—a deliverer—who could provide sustenance, security, and salvation.

Geographical Insight

Jesus and his disciples withdrew to Bethsaida, located near the border of Philip's territory. This move had a strategic advantage: it placed them beyond the immediate jurisdiction of Herod Antipas, who had just executed John the Baptist. The region, known for its proximity to the Sea of Galilee, would soon serve as the stage for an even greater confrontation—Jesus' battle against the primordial enemy of God's order: the Sea.

Tactical Insight

By feeding the 5,000, Jesus established himself as the Provider-King. The miraculous provision of food to a massive crowd echoed the wilderness provision of manna under Moses (Exodus 16). By feeding them, Jesus demonstrated his ability to sustain his people, reinforcing his identity as the one who would shepherd and sustain the true Empire of God.

But the event had another layer of significance. In the ancient world, a king who could provide abundant food was seen as divinely appointed. The crowds recognized this and attempted to force Jesus into kingship (John 6:15). Yet his kingdom was not of this world. Rather than leading a revolt against Rome, Jesus was preparing for a cosmic battle against a greater enemy: Chaos itself.

The famous incident in which Jesus walked on water was the second of the two-part battle between Jesus and the great primordial enemy, Chaos. For the ancient Near Eastern world, the Sea was not just water—it was Chaos incarnate, the physical place inhabited by the terrifying deity of Chaos. It was the realm of the primordial dragon, the domain of Leviathan (Job 41), Yamm (Canaanite myths), and Tiamat (Babylonian myth). Throughout the Hebrew Bible, only Yahweh could tame or trample the waters (Psalm 77:16-19, Isaiah 51:9-10). By walking on the Sea of Galilee, Jesus was doing what only God could do—subjugating Chaos, proving his divine Sonship, and demonstrating his authority over creation itself. The event mirrored the ancient battles between the chief deity and the forces of the abyss, proving that Jesus, as the Son of God, was not merely a teacher or prophet. He was the one sent to defeat the ancient enemy of God and humanity. He was demonstrating to his disciples what they had misinterpreted the first time (Matthew 8), where he battled the Sea and silenced it. But this time, they realized just who he was, as they declared, "Truly this is the Son of God" (Matthew 14:33).

The next day, Jesus issued a theological challenge to the crowd: "I am the bread of life" (John 6:35). His words dismantled their expectations. They wanted a political king who would overthrow Rome and continue feeding them physical bread. But Jesus demanded complete allegiance. Many deserted him, unwilling to follow an empire that did not promise immediate victory but instead demanded absolute loyalty and faith.

Strategic Questions

1. Why did Jesus refuse to become king after the feeding? His kingship was not about military power but divine rule over the world and cosmic forces. His battle was against Sin, Death, and Chaos—not merely Rome.

2. Why did Jesus walk on water? This was not just a miracle. It was a declaration of victory over Chaos, proving his Sonship and divine authority in line with ancient Near Eastern and Hebrew traditions.

3. Why did followers abandon Jesus after the Bread of Life discourse? They expected a messianic warrior but were given a king who demanded faith over force. Many could not reconcile their version of messianic revolution with that which Jesus was establishing. This was Jesus' point, too. While communicating a deep theological point, he was also thinning out his movement. By this point, Jesus knew that he needed followers who had come to a certain level of commitment to his cause.

—SCENE 16—
THE REFINING FIRE

Galilee, Near the Sea, Ituraea | Summer–Fall 28 AD

Campaign Chronology

- **Conflict over Uncleanness |** Mt 15:1-20 | Mk 7:1-23 | Jn 7:1
- **Greek Woman Near Tyre & Sidon |** Mt 15:21-28 | Mk 7:24-30
- **Healings in Region of Decapolis |** Mt 15:29-31 | Mk 7:31-37
- **Feeding of Four Thousand in Region |** Mt 15:32-38 | Mk 8:1-9
- **Return to Galilee, Opposition |** Mt 15:39-16:4 | Mk 8:9-12

- **Warning about Opposition** | Mt 16:5-12 | Mk 8:13-21
- **Healing of Blind Man at Bethsaida** | Mk 8:22-36
- **Peter's Recognition of Jesus in Ituraea** | Mt 16:13-20 | Mk 8:27-30 | Lk 9:18-21
- **Jesus Predicts Passion, Resurrection** | Mt 16:21-26 | Mk 8:31-37 | Lk 9:22-25
- **Jesus' Declaration of Coming Son of Man** | Mt 16:27-28 | Mk 8:38-9:1 | Lk 9:26-27
- **Transfiguration of Jesus (Mt Hermon?)** | Mt 17:1-8 | Mk 9:2-8 | Lk 9:28-36
- **Post-Transfiguration Discussion** | Mt 17:9-13 | Mk 9:9-13 | Lk 9:36
- **Healing of Demon-Possessed Boy** | Mt 17:14-20 | Mk 9:14-29 | Lk 9:37-43
- **Jesus' (2nd) Prediction of Fate** | Mt 17:22-23 | Mk 9:30-32 | Lk 9:43-45

Social, Religious & Political Context

Jesus' rising influence had not gone unnoticed. His continued confrontations with religious authorities intensified the opposition against him. The Pharisees and scribes, who had long monitored his actions, escalated their scrutiny, especially over issues of purity laws, food traditions, and ritual uncleanness. This was not simply theological nitpicking. Purity regulations were central to Jewish identity under Roman rule, and Jesus' deliberate violations of these laws threatened to undermine the established order.

Meanwhile, Herod Antipas remained ever watchful. The execution of John the Baptist had already proven that perceived threats would be swiftly eliminated. As Jesus' movement grew, Herod's concern deepened, particularly with reports that Jesus was being hailed as a new prophet, perhaps even as John resurrected (Mark 6:14-16). The Galilean phase of Jesus' campaign was drawing to a close. If he remained, the confrontation would become unavoidable.

Tactical Insight

Sensing the danger, Jesus took an unexpected turn: he withdrew from Jewish territory entirely, heading into Gentile regions like Tyre, Sidon, and the Decapolis, or "Ten Cities" region (Mark 7:24-37). This was more than just a retreat. It was a test for his disciples. Their nationalistic expectations of the Messiah made it difficult to accept that Jesus' message extended beyond Israel. The episode with the

Syrophoenician woman (Mark 7:24-30) forced them to reckon with the radical inclusivity of the Empire of God. His healings among Gentiles and the second feeding miracle of 4,000 people in a non-Jewish region (Mark 8:1-9) signified that the coming Empire was not confined to Israel alone. Jesus' priority was Empire over nation.

Peter's confession was a turning point in Jesus' public campaign. Upon his return to Jewish territory, Jesus led his disciples north to Caesarea Philippi, a heavily Romanized city with deep pagan significance. Here, in the shadow of shrines dedicated to Caesar and the god Pan, Peter finally understood what the others had failed to see—Jesus was the Messiah (Matthew 16:13-20).

Yet immediately after this breakthrough, Peter faltered. Jesus began speaking of suffering, rejection, and death—ideas completely foreign to traditional messianic expectations. Peter, still clinging to a vision of a conquering warrior king, rebuked Jesus for suggesting such a fate. Jesus' reply was sharp: "Get behind me, Satan!" (Mark 8:33). The conflict was no longer just external, even his closest followers struggled to grasp the true nature of his mission.

As opposition grew, Jesus moved toward Mount Hermon, the site of the Transfiguration (Mark 9:2-8). This was no random event. It was a decisive moment of divine affirmation. Moses and Elijah appeared, symbolizing the Law and the Prophets, validating Jesus as their fulfillment. God's voice thundered from the heavens: "This is my Son; listen to him!" (Mark 9:7). This echoed divine coronation language found in Psalm 2. The setting itself was symbolic. Mount Hermon, in Jewish apocalyptic thought, was the mythological site where rebellious angels descended in the days of Noah (1 Enoch 6:6). This moment was more than a revelation of glory. It was a declaration of war against cosmic forces that had long held the world in bondage.

Strategic Questions

1. Why keep his identity secret? Despite these revelations, Jesus strictly instructed his disciples not to tell anyone about his Messiahship (Mark 9:9-10). A premature declaration would trigger an immediate crackdown. Herod and the Jerusalem authorities would see him as a direct political threat. The people still misunderstood what kind of Messiah he was. They expected a revolutionary leader, not a suffering servant. His war was not against Rome alone—it was against Sin, Death, and Chaos. If the people sought to crown him as a political king in an earthly sense, they would miss the true battle entirely. The phase of open engagement was coming to an end. Now, Jesus turned his eyes toward Jerusalem—the final battleground.

2. Why did Jesus retreat to Gentile territory? By withdrawing from Galilee and venturing into Gentile regions like Tyre, Sidon, and the Decapolis (Mark 7:24-37), Jesus was not merely evading hostile authorities. He was making a profound statement about the scope of his mission. The Jewish expectation was that the Messiah would restore Israel's national glory, yet Jesus' actions challenged this assumption. His encounter with the Syrophoenician woman (Mark 7:24-30) tested the disciples' understanding of God's kingdom. When this Gentile demonstrated greater faith than many of God's people, Jesus affirmed that the blessings of his Empire were not restricted by ethnicity. By healing Gentiles and performing a second mass feeding for 4,000 in a non-Jewish region (Mark 8:1-9), Jesus signaled that the redemption he was bringing extended beyond Israel to the nations.

3. Why did Jesus choose Caesarea Philippi for Peter's confession? Caesarea Philippi was a city steeped in imperial and pagan symbolism. Home to shrines dedicated to Caesar and Pan, it was a site where Rome's power and pagan religion intertwined. By leading his disciples there, Jesus deliberately set the stage for one of the most pivotal moments in his campaign. Peter's declaration—"You are the Messiah" (Matthew 16:16)—was a direct challenge to both Jewish and Roman expectations. Yet Jesus immediately shattered Peter's vision of a military conqueror by predicting his suffering and death. In this setting, where Caesar was worshiped as a god, Jesus revealed the true path of kingship—not through violent conquest, but through self-sacrifice. By choosing this location, Jesus made it clear: his kingdom would not be like the empires of the world, and his mission was far greater than national liberation.

—SCENE 17—
REGROUP & REINFORCE

Regrouping in Capernaum & Defense of the Weak | Galilee, Near the Sea, Ituraea |Fall 28 AD

Campaign Chronology

- **Return to Capernaum |** Mt 17:24-18:35
- **Payment of Temple Tax |** Mt 17:24-27
- **Greatness in the Empire |** Mt 18:1-5 | Mk 9:33-37 | Lk 9:46-48
- **Warning against Harming Children & Others |** Mt 18:6-14 | Mk 9:38-50 | Lk 9:49-50
- **How to Treat a Sinful Sibling |** Mt 18:15-35

Climate & Seasonal Context

As fall set in, the scorching heat of the Galilean summer gave way to cooler temperatures, making travel and public gatherings more manageable. This season of transition mirrored Jesus' own strategy—shifting from regional confrontations to final preparations before the march to Jerusalem. The next phase would not be a mere escalation but a decisive movement into enemy territory.

Geographical Insight

Capernaum, Jesus' operational base, was not just a place of retreat but a staging ground for the next offensive. Unlike Nazareth, which had rejected him, Capernaum provided a mix of Jewish and Roman influences, a perfect setting for shaping the ideology of his disciples. Here, Jesus reinforced the true nature of his Empire, ensuring that his followers were ready for what lay ahead.

Tactical Insight

The Temple tax incident was a key moment in Jesus' campaign. When asked about the Temple tax (Matthew 17:24-27), Jesus used the moment to expose the system's corruption. Rather than rejecting the tax outright—a move that would have made him an easy target—he subtly undermined it. Instructing Peter to retrieve a coin from a fish's mouth, he mocked the religious economy, showing that even nature provided more freely than the Temple elite. This wasn't just about taxation. It was a critique of a system profiting off God's people.

In redefining leadership rules, Jesus asserted that the greatest must become the least. The disciples, still thinking in worldly terms, argued over who was the greatest (Mark 9:33-37). Jesus shattered their assumptions by placing a child before them—a symbol of humility and powerlessness in their society. True leadership in God's Empire would not be about status or control, but servanthood. Those seeking power for themselves had no place in his movement.

Mercy, that is, forgiveness and protecting the weak, was highly scandalous. Jesus followed with teachings on forgiveness and responsibility (Matthew 18:6-35), warning against harming the "little ones." Unlike human society, where the weak were discarded, Jesus' Empire—which spanned both heaven and earth—defended them with the fiercest of heavenly warriors. The parable of the unmerciful servant (Matthew 18:23-35) made clear that forgiveness was not weakness. It was warfare against oppression, revenge, and the power.

Strategic Questions

1. Why not march to Jerusalem yet? The disciples weren't ready. They still misunderstood power and leadership, expecting conquest rather than servanthood. Jesus had to reshape their thinking before they faced the full pressure of Rome and the Temple elite. The final march required absolute commitment, and they had to learn that the battle wasn't just external—it was within their own hearts.

2. Why did Jesus use a child to illustrate greatness in his Empire? In first-century Jewish and Roman society, children held little social status or power. They were dependent, vulnerable, and had no legal standing. By placing a child in their midst and declaring that the greatest must become like them (Matthew 18:1-5), Jesus completely inverted their understanding of leadership. His disciples were still thinking in terms of hierarchy and dominance, expecting that power in God's Empire would function like it did in earthly kingdoms. But Jesus redefined greatness as humility, dependence on God, and self-giving service. This lesson was crucial as they neared Jerusalem, where their ideas of power would be fully tested. To follow Jesus was not to climb the ranks of an elite movement, but to descend into servanthood, sacrifice, and suffering—as he would demonstrate.

3. Why did Jesus link children to the most powerful angels in heaven? In Matthew 18:10, Jesus makes an extraordinary claim: "See that you do not despise one of these little ones. For I tell you that their angels in heaven always see the face of my Father in heaven." At first glance, this may seem like a simple reassurance that children are under divine care. But in the context of ancient Jewish tradition, Jesus is saying something far more radical. The phrase "their angels" suggests not just any heavenly beings, but the most exalted angelic figures—the Angels of the Face—who, in Jewish thought, stood in the immediate presence of God. These were not ordinary messengers or warrior angels but the highest-ranking beings in heaven, and the only beings in the entire heavenly world powerful enough to withstand being in God's immediate presence without being destroyed. By saying that these are the angels assigned to watch over children, Jesus was making a staggering point: in the divine order, the weakest and most vulnerable in human society are attended by the highest-ranking celestial beings. This statement also carried an implicit warning: to harm or disregard a child is to oppose the very will of God, for they are under the care of his closest angelic servants. In Jesus' Empire, power belonged to those whom the world considered powerless. The protection of the weak was not optional—it was woven into the very fabric of the divine order.

There's No Turning Back

The revolution had reached its most dangerous stage. Jesus was no longer a rising figure in Galilee but a direct threat to the power structures of Jerusalem. This phase was marked by bold, confrontational tactics as Jesus moved into enemy territory. He did not come in secret. He entered Jerusalem for Sukkot, a festival loaded with political and messianic overtones. He taught openly in the Temple, debated the religious elite, and exposed their hypocrisy before the masses. He forced them to act, escalating the conflict to the point of no return.

But this was not just an earthly battle. As Jesus waged war against Rome's collaborators, he also went on the offensive against Sin, Death, and the forces of Chaos. He demonstrated his supreme authority by healing the blind, raising the dead, and teaching of an Empire where the last would be first and the powerful would be overthrown. His resurrection of Lazarus was the ultimate act of defiance—proof that even Death could not stand against him.

Yet, the cost of this insurgency was rising. The Sanhedrin was actively plotting his execution. Spies infiltrated his gatherings. His disciples began to feel the weight of the movement, questioning their own commitment. The Empire was advancing, but so was the opposition. The final confrontation was growing near. Jerusalem was no longer a place of teaching but a battlefield. The revolution was at a tipping point, and at this point, there was no turning back.

—SCENE 18—
THE COUNTEROFFENSIVE

Journey to Jerusalem for Sukkot | Galilee to Jerusalem | Fall 28 AD

Campaign Chronology

- **Ridicule by Jesus' Siblings | Jn 7:2-9**
- **On way to Jerusalem through Samaria | Lk 9:51-56 | Jn 7:10**
- **Complete Commitment Required | Mt 8:19-22 | Lk 9:57-62**
- **In Jerusalem for Sukkot**
  - **Reactions to Jesus' Teaching, Miracles | Jn 7:11-31**
  - **Attempt to Arrest Jesus | Jn 7:32-52**
  - **Woman Caught in Adultery | Jn 7:53-8:11**

Social, Religious & Political Context

Sukkot, the Feast of Tabernacles, was one of the most politically charged festivals in Jerusalem. It commemorated Israel's time in the wilderness but also carried deep messianic expectations— expectations that often fueled anti-Roman sentiment. With the city filled with tens of thousands of Jewish pilgrims, Roman forces increased their presence, wary of unrest. The Sanhedrin and Temple authorities also watched closely, fearing that any perceived messianic figure could incite rebellion.

Jesus' decision to go to Jerusalem during this festival was not just an act of religious devotion. It was a calculated move to confront the powers head-on. If his movement was to challenge the existing order, he had to step directly into enemy territory.

Tactical Insight

At first, Jesus stayed away, knowing that his presence in Jerusalem made him a target (John 7:1-10). Even his own brothers mocked him, urging him to go publicly and prove himself. But Jesus wasn't seeking spectacle—he moved deliberately. He arrived in the city discreetly and only later revealed himself in the most public and provocative way possible: by teaching in the Temple.

By standing in the Temple courts and teaching (John 7:14-31), Jesus was making a bold statement. The Temple was the center of Jewish religious and political life, controlled by the elite priestly class. To preach there, uninvited and unsanctioned, was an act of defiance.

Crowds marveled at his words, wondering how someone with no formal rabbinic training could speak with such authority. The religious leaders quickly moved to discredit him, questioning his legitimacy. But Jesus turned their attacks back on them, accusing them of hypocrisy and exposing their corruption. His words resonated with the people, deepening the rift between himself and the Temple elite.

Jesus' remarks on water and light served as a theological power play. Sukkot featured two major Temple rituals. One was the Water-Pouring Ceremony, symbolizing God's provision and the hope of the Holy Spirit. The other was the Festival of Lights, where massive menorahs were lit, representing God's guidance and presence.

Jesus deliberately tied his teaching to these symbols at their most climactic moments. These declarations enraged the authorities, escalating their efforts to silence him. At one moment, Jesus declared: "If anyone is thirsty, let him come to me" (John 7:37-39). As the priests poured water at the altar, Jesus stood up and declared that he, not the Temple, was the true source of living water. This statement linked him to prophetic promises of salvation and directly challenged the religious system's claim to mediate God's presence. And he maintained: "I am the Light of the World" (John 8:12). During the lighting of the great menorahs, Jesus proclaimed himself as the true Light—the one who leads people out of darkness (Isaiah 9:2). This was an unmistakable claim to divine authority and a direct challenge to the religious establishment.

The authorities struck back at Jesus in their attempts to arrest and kill him. Unable to discredit him in debate, the Temple leaders sent guards to arrest him (John 7:32-46). But even they returned empty-handed, amazed by his words: "No one ever spoke like this man!" The failure to detain him only fueled their desperation. Later, in a heated confrontation, Jesus accused them of being sons of the devil, not of God (John 8:42-47). This was the breaking point. They attempted to stone him on the spot (John 8:58-59), but he escaped—his time had not yet come.

Strategic Question

1. Why confront the Temple authorities in their stronghold? For three key reasons. One, to expose their corruption. As long as they controlled the Temple, they controlled the people. By directly engaging them, Jesus tore down their false authority. Two, to force a decisive confrontation. Jesus was no longer avoiding conflict—he was accelerating it. By openly teaching in the Temple during a politically charged festival, he ensured the battle lines were drawn. Three, to redefine access to God. The Temple had become a place of economic and spiritual exploitation. Jesus positioned himself as the new access point to the Father. This was no longer a mere debate. The ruling class wasn't just challenging Jesus. They were now actively plotting his death. His war with the authorities had entered its final phase, and the road to the cross had begun.

From Sukkot to Hanukkah| Jerusalem, Around Judea | Fall–Winter 28 AD

Campaign Chronology

- **Commissioning of Seventy** | Lk 10:17-24
- **Good Samaritan** | Lk 10:25-37
- **Visit with Mary & Martha** | Lk 10:38-42
- **Lesson on Prayer, Parable of Bold Friend** | Lk 11:1-13
- **Debate with Opponents** | Lk 11:14-36
- **Woe to Opponents, Meal with Pharisee** | Lk 11:37-54
- **Warning to Twelve against Hypocrisy** | Lk 12:1-12
- **Warning about Greed, Trust in Wealth** | Lk 12:13-34
- **On Being Unprepared for Son of Man** | Lk 12:35-48
- **Warning about Coming Division** | Lk 12:49-53
- **On Lacking Discernment about Present** | Lk 12:54-59
- **Either Repent or Perish** | Lk 13:1-9
- **Healing, Opposition on Sabbath** | Lk 13:10-21
- **Attempted Stoning, Arrest at Hanukkah** | Jn 10:22-39

Social, Religious & Political Context

Hanukkah was more than just a religious festival. It was a reminder of Jewish resistance against foreign rule. It commemorated the Maccabean revolt (167–160 BC), when Jewish fighters led by Judah Maccabee overthrew the Seleucid oppressors and reclaimed the Temple. In Jesus' time, the festival carried strong nationalistic overtones, stirring hope for another liberator to rise against Rome.

For Jesus to remain in Jerusalem during Hanukkah, teaching openly in the Temple (John 10:22-39), was a direct challenge to Jewish and Roman authorities. His presence in Solomon's Colonnade—a space associated with King David's dynasty—signaled a bold claim. The people demanded clarity: Was he the Messiah? Would he lead the revolt? His response would either rally the crowds or seal his fate.

Tactical Insight

As opposition mounted in Jerusalem, Jesus sent seventy disciples throughout the land (Luke 10:1-24). This was not just about preaching. It was an escalation of his movement. By sending them in pairs before, he was spreading his message strategically while avoiding immediate suppression. Now, he knew that he needed to increase his reach by sending even more of his followers out. The number seventy symbolized all the nations of the world (Genesis 10), hinting that his mission was expanding beyond Israel.

Jesus' teachings of fire and division made it clear that neutrality was no longer an option. At this point in his campaign, his teachings became sharper, more urgent. He warned of fire, judgment, and the cost of following him (Luke 12:49-53). He condemned greed (Luke 12:13-34), religious hypocrisy (Luke 12:1-12), and spiritual complacency (Luke 12:35-48). His words made one thing clear: there was no room for halfhearted disciples. People had to choose—join the movement or stand against it.

Jesus continued his attacks on the Pharisees, publicly exposing their corruption at a dinner gathering (Luke 11:37-54). He accused them of being outwardly pious but inwardly rotten, misleading the people rather than shepherding them. This was not just theological criticism but an outright declaration of war on the establishment.

The leaders' attempt to stone Jesus during Hanukkah was a breaking point. During Hanukkah, Jesus stood in Solomon's Colonnade, and the people pressed him: Was he the Messiah? His response? "I and the Father are one." The reaction? They tried to stone him on the spot. This was the tipping point. The authorities were no longer concerned with debate or trapping him in legal technicalities. They wanted him eliminated.

Strategic Questions

1. Why remain in Jerusalem for Hanukkah? Hanukkah was a festival of national pride and messianic expectation. Teaching in the Temple at this time forced the people to confront the question: Was Jesus the long-awaited deliverer?

2. Why escalate the movement by sending out seventy disciples? Jesus was not waiting for conflict to find him—he was expanding his reach. The more people who embraced his message, the harder it would be for the authorities to suppress him quietly.

3. Why did the religious leaders react so violently during Hanukkah? Jesus' claim to be one with the Father was more than blasphemy. It was a direct challenge to their authority. If the people believed him, the Temple system would collapse, and their power would be gone.

From Hanukkah to Week of Passover 3 | Perea, Judean Desert, Samaria, Jerusalem | Winter 28–Spring 29 AD

Campaign Chronology

- **From Jerusalem to Perea** | Jn 10:40-42
- **On Entering the Empire** | Lk 13:22-30
- **Challenge to Herod, Sorry for Jerusalem** | Lk 13:31-35
- *At the Perean Pharisee's House* | Lk 14:1-24
  - **Healing of Man with Dropsy** | Lk 14:1-6
  - **Parable of Great Banquet** | Lk 14:7-24
- **Cost of Discipleship** | Lk 14:25-35
- **On Associating with Sinners** | Lk 15:1-32
- **Parable on Proper Use of Money** | Lk 16:1-13
- **Condemnation of Wealth** | Lk 16:14-31
- **Four Lessons on Discipleship** | Lk 17:1-10
- **Death of Lazarus in Bethany** | Jn 11:1-16
- **Raising of Lazarus from the Dead** | Jn 11:17-44
- **Sanhedrin's Decision to Kill Jesus** | Jn 11:45-53
- **Withdrawal, Reconvening with Disciples** | Jn 11:54
- **Healing of Lepers Near Samaria, Galilee** | Lk 17:11-21
- **On the Coming of the Son of Man** | Lk 17:22-37
- **Parable on Persistent Prayer** | Lk 18:1-14
- **Conflict with Opposition about Divorce** | Mt 19:1-12 | Mk 10:1-12
- **Little Children & the Empire** | Mt 19:13-15 | Mk 10:13-15 | Lk 18:15-17
- **Riches & the Empire** | Mt 19:16-30 | Mk 10:17-31 | Lk 18:18-30
- **Parable of the Sovereign Landowner** | Mt 20:1-16
- **Prediction (3rd) of Death, Resurrection** | Mt 20:17-19 | Mk 10:32-34 | Lk 18:31-34
- **Warning against Pride** | Mt 20:20-28 | Mk 10:35-45
- **Healing of Blind Bartimaeus, Companion** | Mt 20:29-34 | Mk 10:46-52 | Lk 18:35-43
- **Zaccheus** | Lk 19:1-10
- **Parable on Awaiting the Empire** | Lk 19:11-28

Social, Religious & Political Context

With Jesus' movement now at its peak, the Sanhedrin had made its decision to assassinate him. The Lazarus resurrection had confirmed his threat level, and now spies were embedded in his gatherings (Luke 20:20), seeking evidence to use against him. Every public action, every teaching, every move was being watched.

The shift in strategy was clear: Jesus had to prepare his followers for what was coming. The revolution was about to enter its most dangerous phase, and not all who followed him would endure.

Tactical Insight

During this phase, Jesus' teachings became sharper, more challenging, and deeply counter-cultural. He tested the loyalty of his followers, forcing them to decide whether they were willing to embrace the full cost of his movement.

Then came Jesus' most provocative act yet—the resurrection of Lazarus (John 11:1-44). Raising the dead was more than just a miracle. It was an unmistakable messianic sign. In Jewish thought, only God had power over life and death. While Elijah and Elisha had resurrected people, they had done so by invoking God's power. Jesus, however, commanded Lazarus to rise by his own authority. This was a direct claim to divine status. And in calling Lazarus out of the earth-hewn tomb, Jesus was effectively rescuing Lazarus from the insatiable appetite of Death and declaring outright war against the primordial forces of Death. The reaction was immediate. The miracle electrified Jerusalem, and the leaders panicked. If Jesus continued unchecked, the entire city would follow him. The Sanhedrin met in crisis mode and made a decision: Jesus had to die. From that moment, they formally plotted his execution (John 11:45-53).

The parable of the rich man and Lazarus (Luke 16:19-31) made it clear that wealth and power had no place in his Empire unless they were used for justice. Jesus' encounter with the rich young ruler (Luke 18:18-30) exposed the real issue. Money wasn't just an obstacle—it was a rival lord. Jesus' challenge was set: Would people choose comfort or commitment?

Jesus' association with Zacchaeus was a direct challenge to the economic system. In Jericho, Jesus invited himself into the home of Zacchaeus, a chief tax collector (Luke 19:1-10). This was not just a meal. It was a public act of defiance. Zacchaeus was part of Rome's economic exploitation system, but after meeting Jesus, he vowed to give away half his wealth and repay fourfold what he had taken unjustly. This was an example of what true repentance looked like.

Changing inwardly and repairing the damage done for one's behavior. It was an economic reversal—an example of Jesus Empire.

Jesus warned his disciples that suffering was coming (Luke 18:31-34). The movement wasn't about securing earthly power. It was about overthrowing the cosmic forces that enslaved humanity. He predicted his death a third time, but his disciples still struggled to grasp the reality—they were expecting a political triumph, not a suffering king.

Jesus' final miracles demonstrated his ultimate authority. As Jesus approached Jerusalem, he healed blind Bartimaeus (Luke 18:35-43), another symbolic act. He was opening the eyes of those ready to see the truth. The parable of the ten minas (Luke 19:11-27) emphasized loyalty in the face of risk—not everyone would remain faithful.

Strategic Question

1. Why focus on wealth at this stage? It was the last dividing line. Jesus knew that many followed him for miracles and teachings, but true discipleship required forsaking all earthly attachments. It exposed the corrupt foundation of society. His movement wasn't just about personal salvation. It was outward and collective as well. It was about overthrowing the unjust systems that exploited the poor. It set the standard for leadership. His Empire would not be ruled by the rich, the powerful, or the elite, but by those who embodied radical generosity, humility, and service. It forced a choice before the final battle. His followers needed to understand that once they entered Jerusalem, there would be no turning back. By the end of this phase, the battle lines were fully drawn. Jesus had purged his movement of halfhearted followers and prepared his disciples for what was ahead.

2. Why raise Lazarus if it would lead to his own death? Demonstrating power over Death was the ultimate proof of Jesus' authority, but it also sealed his fate. In the old cosmic order, a life reclaimed meant a life owed. Death had a claim, and if Lazarus was to be freed from its grip, a sacrifice had to be made in his place. By calling Lazarus out of the grave, Jesus was not just performing a miracle—he was issuing a direct challenge to Death's dominion, forcing a confrontation that could not be avoided. But Jesus knew the cost. He willingly became the offering, the one who would be handed over in exchange. His decision set in motion the final showdown—not just with the authorities who would condemn him, but with Death itself. The Sanhedrin, believing they were eliminating a political threat, unknowingly became agents in the very plan Jesus had orchestrated all along. In seeking to destroy him, they carried out the great exchange—one man dying so that others might be free of enslavement to the perverse and insatiable appetites of Death.

The Insurgent Empire Fails. Then Prevails

The insurgency reached its climax. The march into Jerusalem was no mere procession. It was a calculated strike at the heart of the oppressive order. Jesus entered the city as a king, not on a warhorse, but on a donkey, fulfilling Zechariah's prophecy and declaring an Empire unlike any Rome had seen. The people hailed him, but the authorities prepared to silence him.

This was the moment of reckoning. Jesus seized control of the Temple, the economic and religious stronghold of the corrupt elite, making his boldest move yet. His words cut deep—parables and debates exposed the hypocrisy of the leaders. Every action forced a response. The plot against him was tightening.

Yet, this battle was being fought on two fronts. In the cosmic realm, Jesus was not just toppling the powers of Rome—he was challenging Death itself. The trial, the brutal execution, the mocking crown of thorns—these were the enemy's last desperate attempts to maintain control. But the cross did not defeat him; it enthroned him.

And then, the unthinkable. The tomb was empty. The final enemy, Death, has been vanquished, as Jesus escaped its hungry maw in glorious fashion. The true Empire had been launched—not through military conquest, but through resurrection. The movement that should have ended in despair instead exploded outward, unstoppable. The war had been won, and the Empire of God had begun.

—SCENE 21—
THE MARCH ON JERUSALEM

Week of Passover 3 | Bethany, Jerusalem, In the Temple | Spring 29 AD

Campaign Chronology

- **Jesus' Arrival at Bethany before Passover |** Jn 11:55-12:11
- **Triumphal Entry into Jerusalem |** Mt 21:1-17 | Mk 11:1-11 | Lk 19:29-44 | Jn 12:12-19
- **Return to Bethany for Night |** Mt 21:17 | Mk 11:11
- **Cursing of Fig Tree on way to Jerusalem |** Mt 21:18-19 | Mk 11:12-14
- **Second Strike Against the Temple |** Mt 21:12-13 | Mk 11:15-18 | Lk 19:45-48

- **Greeks See Jesus, Son of Man Lifted Up** | Jn 12:20-36
- **Jesus & the Crowds** | Jn 12:36-50
- **Withered Fig Tree & Faith** | Mt 21:19-22 | Mk 11:19-25 | Lk 21:37-38
- **Opponents Challenge Jesus' Authority** | Mt 21:23-27 | Mk 11:27-33 | Lk 20:1-8
- **Jesus' Riposte, Question, Parables** | Mt 21:28-22:14 | Mk 12:1-12 | Lk 20:9-19
- **Opponents' Challenge Jesus on Taxes** | Mt 22:15-22 | Mk 12:13-17 | Lk 20:20-26
- **Sadducees' Question about Resurrection** | Mt 22:23-33 | Mk 12:18-27 | Lk 20:27-40
- **Pharisees' Question about Law** | Mt 22:34-40 | Mk 12:28-34
- **Jesus' Riposte, Question about Messiah** | Mt 22:41-46 | Mk 12:35-37 | Lk 20:41-44
- **Seven Woes against Opponents** | Mt 23:1-36 | Mk 12:38-40 | Lk 20:45-47
- **Jesus' Sorrow over Jerusalem** | Mt 23:37-39
- **Widow's Mite** | Mk 12:41-44 | Lk 21:1-4

Climate & Seasonal Context

Spring in Jerusalem brought warm days (60–75°F) with cooler nights, ideal for mass gatherings as pilgrims flooded the city for Passover. The dry season had begun, making roads more accessible and ensuring that the massive influx of people could travel and assemble freely. The festival atmosphere was electric, as Jewish nationalism surged during this sacred time of deliverance—a dangerous mix under Roman rule.

Geographical Insight

Bethany served as Jesus' base of operations, a quiet refuge just outside Jerusalem where he could retreat after days of public confrontation. Located two miles east of the city, it allowed for strategic regrouping with his disciples, while still keeping him within striking distance of the Temple.

Jerusalem itself was the nerve center of Jewish religious and political life—the site where Jesus would stage his most provocative and disruptive actions. The Temple Mount, the heart of Israel's religious system, was already under heavy Roman and priestly surveillance, especially during Passover. Any messianic figure stirring up the crowds risked swift intervention.

Social, Religious & Political Context

Passover drew tens upon tens of thousands of pilgrims, many of whom carried long-simmering hopes for deliverance from Roman rule. The festival itself was a loaded symbol of liberation, celebrating Israel's exodus from Egypt, while also amplifying present-day cries for freedom. The religious elite and Roman authorities were on edge. Pilate and the Sanhedrin closely monitored for insurrection, as radical movements often used Passover to incite rebellion.

Jesus' growing reputation had made him a marked man among the Pharisees, Sadducees, and Roman officials. By entering Jerusalem riding on a donkey (Zechariah 9:9)—a clear messianic declaration—Jesus forced the issue. The crowds hailed him as "Son of David," placing him in opposition to both the Temple elite and Rome itself.

Tactical Insight

Jesus' entrance into the city was a calculated political and prophetic act. By choosing a donkey instead of a warhorse, he mocked imperial power, presenting his Kingdom as an anti-Empire, one built on justice rather than domination. The palm branches and hosannas shouted by the crowds were more than praise. They were symbols of defiance, signaling that Jesus was the liberator they had been waiting for.

The second strike on the Temple was a direct assault against the social, religious, political, and economic elite. This was not a mere protest against commerce in the Temple. It was a dismantling of the entire system that had turned the Temple into an economic stronghold rather than a place of divine encounter. Jesus' act sent shockwaves through the Sanhedrin, forcing them to accelerate their plot to assassinate him as his influence spiraled beyond their control.

Strategic Questions

1. Why stage the Triumphal Entry? Jesus' entry into Jerusalem was a calculated move to force the hand of both religious and political authorities. Riding in on a donkey (Matthew 21:1-11) was not just a fulfillment of Zechariah 9:9. It was a direct challenge to Rome's and the Temple elite's authority. His procession also echoed the ancient Mesopotamian enthronement of Ninurta, the divine warrior-son of the chief god, who entered cities in triumphant processions to be recognized as ruler and bringer of divine justice. In this light, Jesus was presenting himself as the Son of God—not just in the Jewish sense, but in a way that spoke to an even older tradition of divine kingship. The people's cries of "Hosanna!" echoed royal acclaim, but Jesus knew their expectations were misplaced. They longed for a warrior king

who would violently (and merely) overthrow Rome, but his mission was to unseat the deeper enemies—Sin and Death. His entry was not just a march toward the throne. It was a march toward the cross, the true coronation where his kingship would be revealed in full.

2. Why strike the Temple a second time? Jesus' attack on the Temple (Matthew 21:12-13) was not just an act of protest against economic corruption. It was a symbolic declaration that the current system was finished. The Temple, meant to be a house of prayer for "all people," had become a stronghold of exploitation, enriching the elite while oppressing the poor. This second confrontation, coming at the height of Passover preparations, was more than a repeat of his earlier challenge—it was an escalation. By overturning tables and driving out merchants, Jesus was doing what the prophets had long warned: denouncing a religious order that had strayed from God's true purposes. But there was more at stake. In the ancient world, a Temple was the seat of divine power. By disrupting its operations, Jesus was declaring that God's presence was no longer tied to that structure. As he'd done two years earlier, he declared here again that the true Temple was now found in him. This was not just a rebuke. It was a warning that the entire system would soon fall, both spiritually and—within a generation—physically, as Rome would raze the Temple to the ground in 70 AD.

3. Why use Passover as the moment for escalation? Passover was the most volatile time in Jerusalem, filled with nationalistic fervor and memories of Israel's liberation from Egypt. Worshippers flooded the city, and Roman authorities were on high alert, fearing any spark that could ignite a rebellion. By choosing this moment for his final confrontation, Jesus was ensuring that his message and actions would have maximum visibility. But it was more than just a strategic moment—it was theologically loaded. Passover was the festival of deliverance, and Jesus was about to enact the ultimate deliverance, not from Rome, but from Sin and Death. The timing was no accident. As Israel prepared to sacrifice its lambs, Jesus positioned himself as the true Passover Lamb, the one whose blood would mark the path to ultimate salvation. In doing so, he was redefining the festival itself— not as a remembrance of Egypt, but as the inauguration of the new Exodus, one that would lead humanity out of the bondage of Sin and into the Empire of God.

4. Why return to Bethany at night? Despite the day's confrontations, Jesus did not remain in Jerusalem overnight. Instead, he withdrew to Bethany, just outside the city, staying in the home of his supporters (Matthew 21:17). This was not an act of fear but a

tactical move. By leaving the city each night, Jesus controlled the pace of events. He did not allow himself to be cornered or arrested prematurely. Jerusalem was a powder keg during Passover, and the Temple authorities would have preferred to seize him quietly, away from the crowds. By retreating to Bethany, Jesus ensured that his public appearances would remain in the daylight, maximizing their impact and making it clear that his confrontation with the authorities would be on his terms, not theirs. Each return to the city was another calculated move, leading to the inevitable clash that would define the fate of both Jesus and Jerusalem.

—SCENE 22—
WARNINGS, PLOTS & BETRAYALS

From the Temple to the Mount of Olives | Jerusalem, Mount of Olives, Bethany | Spring 29 AD

Campaign Chronology

- **Setting of the Discourse** | Mt 24:1-3 | Mk 13:1-4 | Lk 21:5-7
- **Abomination of Desolation** | Mt 24:15-28 | Mk 13:14-23 | Lk 21:20-24
- **Visitation of the Son of Man** | Mt 24:29-31 | Mk 13:24-27 | Lk 21:25-27
- **The Time is Near but Unknown** | Mt 24:32-41 | Mk 13:28-32 | Lk 21:28-33
- **Parables on Being Watchful, Faithful** | Mt 24:42-25:30 | Mk 13:33-37 | Lk 21:34-36
- **Judgment at Coming of Son of Man** | Mt 25:31-46
- **Plot to Arrest Jesus, High Priest's Palace** | Mt 26:1-5 | Mk 14:1-2 | Lk 22:1-2
- **Jesus Anointed by Mary in Bethany** | Mt 26:6-13 | Mk 14:3-9 | Jn 12:2-8
- **Judas Agrees to Betray Jesus** | Mt 26:14-16 | Mk 14:10-11 | Lk 22:3-6

Climate & Seasonal Context

Spring in Jerusalem meant warm days (60–75°F) with dry conditions, making it perfect for extended public teaching and movement between key locations. The lack of rain allowed for large gatherings in the Temple courtyards and open areas like the Mount of Olives, where Jesus delivered his final teachings. The season also signaled the start of agricultural harvests, a fitting metaphor for Jesus' warnings about the impending judgment and the "harvesting" of the righteous and wicked.

Geographical Insight

The Temple Mount was the epicenter of Jewish worship and authority, the one place where God's presence was believed to dwell. Every action Jesus took here—teaching, debating, and confronting the religious elite—carried massive political and theological implications. His parables and public rebukes within the Temple weren't just moral lessons. They were a direct assault on the corrupt religious system.

The Mount of Olives, just east of Jerusalem, provided a strategic retreat from the city's tensions. It was also deeply messianic territory. Zechariah 14:4 prophesied that God would stand on this mountain at the end of days, bringing divine judgment. Jesus' choice of this location for his final teachings was no accident. It was a statement of sovereignty, preparing his disciples for the coming storm.

Social, Religious & Political Context

By this stage, Jerusalem was divided over Jesus. Many hailed him as the Messiah, while the Sanhedrin saw him as an existential threat. The high priest Caiaphas and his council had already begun plotting his death. The cleansing of the Temple, his public parables condemning religious hypocrisy, and his growing messianic following left them no choice but to act before Passover ended.

Meanwhile, Jesus' warnings about Jerusalem's destruction (the "Abomination of Desolation") had a profoundly political edge. Rome had already crushed Jewish revolts before, suggesting that if Israel continued rejecting the way of peace, divine judgment (and military disaster) would follow. This message struck at the heart of Jewish identity—could God's chosen people really face destruction?

Tactical Insight

The Mount of Olives discourse (Matthew 24, Mark 13, Luke 21) was a battlefield briefing, not just an abstract sermon. Jesus was telling his followers what to expect, how to prepare, and how to endure the coming trials. His parables of watchfulness (the Ten Virgins, the Talents, the Sheep and Goats) were warnings: the Kingdom was arriving, and there would be no neutral ground.

Meanwhile, in the shadows, Judas Iscariot had made his choice. Likely disillusioned by Jesus' refusal to lead a violent rebellion, he struck a deal with the high priest's men. The price? Thirty pieces of silver—the value of a slave (Exodus 21:32). The revolution was at a breaking point, and betrayal was now a part of the script.

Strategic Questions

1. Why deliver final teachings from the Mount of Olives? This location had deep messianic significance, and by teaching there, Jesus was aligning himself with prophetic expectations of divine judgment and renewal.

2. Why use apocalyptic language? Jesus framed the coming conflict in cosmic terms, ensuring that his followers understood this was not just a political struggle. It was the climax of God's plan.

3. Why allow Judas to remain? Jesus had foreseen the betrayal but let it unfold, knowing his arrest would trigger the final confrontation that would lead to the ultimate victory. As the Meal progressed, Jesus identified Judas as his betrayer (John 13:21-30). Yet he did not stop him because the betrayal was part of the plan. The enemy had moved its pieces into place, and the final battle was about to begin.

4. Why warn about Jerusalem's destruction? Jesus' warnings about Jerusalem's coming destruction were not just predictions of doom. They were a final plea for repentance. He saw the city's fate unfolding, not only in a spiritual sense but also in the stark reality of its political and military trajectory. Decades of resistance against Rome were building toward an inevitable catastrophe, and Jesus knew that if the Jews continued on its path—rejecting peace and embracing violent revolution—the city would be crushed. His lament over Jerusalem (Luke 19:41-44) was both sorrowful and strategic, calling the people to recognize the true nature of God's kingdom before it was too late. But they refused to listen. By rejecting him, they were rejecting the only path to salvation, both in the theological sense and in the political sense. In 70 AD, just as he had foretold, Jerusalem was utterly destroyed by the Romans. The warning had been clear, but the leaders and people chose rebellion over repentance, sealing their own fate.

—SCENE 23—
THE KING'S VIGIL

Passover Meal, Final Retreat | Jerusalem, Upper Room, Mount of Olives | Spring 29 AD

Campaign Chronology

- **Preparation for Passover Meal |** Mt 26:17-19 | Mk 14:12-16 | Lk 22:7-13
- **Beginning of Passover Meal |** Mt 26:20 | Mk 14:17 | Lk 22:14-16
- **Jesus Washes the Feet of the Twelve |** Jn 13:1-20

- **Judas Identified as Betrayer** | Mt 26:21-25 | Mk 14:18-21 | Lk 22:21-23 | Jn 13:21-30
- **Argument Among the Twelve** | Lk 22:24-30
- **Closing of the Meal, Lord's Supper** | Mt 26:26-29 | Mk 14:22-25 | Lk 22:17-20
- **Retreat to the Mount of Olives** | Mt 26:30 | Mk 14:26 | Jn 13:30
- **Jesus Predicts Peter's Denial** | Jn 13:31-36
- **Jesus Predicts Twelve will Abandon Him** | Mt 26:31-35 | Mk 14:27-31 | Lk 22:31-38 | Jn 13:37-38
- **On Jesus' Fate, the Father, Holy Spirit** | Jn 14:1-31
- **Vine & Branches** | Jn 15:1-17
- **World Hates Jesus, His Followers** | Jn 15:18-16:4
- **Coming of Holy Spirit** | Jn 16:5-15
- **Prediction, Joy over Jesus' Resurrection** | Jn 16:16-22
- **Promise of Answered Prayer, Peace** | Jn 16:23-33
- **Jesus' Prayer for Twelve, All Followers** | Jn 17:1-26

Tactical Insight

The Passover Meal (*Seder*) was more than a meal. It was a final war council. Jesus redefined the Passover, shifting its focus from the Exodus to his impending sacrifice. He was the new Passover lamb, the one whose blood would mark his followers as those who belonged to the true Empire of God. This was not just a farewell dinner. It was the inauguration of a new covenant, one that would be ratified not by animal sacrifice, but by his own death.

Before the meal, Jesus performed a shocking act of humility: washing the feet of his disciples (John 13:1-20). This was a direct inversion of hierarchy, a lesson in servant leadership. In the empires of this world, kings were served. In Jesus' Empire, the king serves. But this act was also an offensive strike against the disciples' expectations of power. They still anticipated a violent revolution, but Jesus was showing them that the path to victory was through self-sacrifice.

The Garden of Gethsemane became a place of strategic retreat. After the meal, Jesus led his disciples to the Mount of Olives, specifically to the Garden of Gethsemane (Matthew 26:36-46). This was not a random choice, as Gethsemane was an olive grove, a place of pressing, crushing, and extraction. Fittingly, this would be where Jesus would feel the full weight of his mission pressing down on him.

In ancient warfare, commanders would often withdraw before battle for final prayers and preparations. This was Jesus' moment of final readiness, but also of deep agony. He prayed three times, each time returning to find his disciples asleep—a clear indication that they were still unprepared for what was coming. The storm was at the gates, and his closest followers could not stay awake.

Yet, Jesus did not run. He remained in a known location, making no attempt to hide. He knew Judas would lead the authorities here. He wasn't captured—he surrendered. His act of non-resistance was a strategic move: he would let the enemy think they were in control. But the real war was being fought on a different battlefield.

Strategic Questions

1. Why remain in a known location? Jesus was not fleeing from fate—he was walking into it. Gethsemane was no secret hideout. It was a place where Jesus and his disciples regularly gathered. He could have chosen to evade arrest, but instead he positioned himself exactly where he knew Judas would find him. This was not passivity but an act of submission to the divine plan. By remaining in plain sight, Jesus demonstrated that his mission was unfolding according to purpose, not chance.

2. Why did Jesus allow Judas to betray him? The betrayal was not an accident. It was part of the strategy. Jesus knew that his arrest would set the next stage in motion, triggering the events that would lead to the cross. Judas' actions, though treacherous, were not outside of God's plan. Jesus had repeatedly spoken of being "handed over," and now he willingly allowed it to happen. The moment of betrayal wasn't just about Judas. It was about Jesus embracing the road to sacrifice.

3. What did the Last Supper accomplish? It established the new covenant and permanently reshaped Passover. For centuries, Passover had commemorated Israel's deliverance from Egypt, but Jesus now centered it on himself. The bread and wine were no longer just symbols of past liberation. They represented his body and blood, the sacrifice that would bring true and final deliverance. In this meal, Jesus redefined the covenant, marking his death as the moment that would inaugurate the Empire of God.

4. Why did Jesus rebuke Peter's resistance? Because his Empire was not built on violence, but on the willing surrender of power for the sake of others. When Peter drew his sword to fight, he was operating by the world's standards of power—believing that victory must come through force. But Jesus' kingdom was built on an entirely different foundation. He told Peter to put the sword away because this was not a battle won through bloodshed, but through sacrifice. True power came through laying one's life down, not taking another's.

Retreat to the Garden of Gethsemane | Jerusalem, Gethsemane, Mount of Olives | Spring 29 AD

Campaign Chronology

- **Jesus Retreats to Gethsemane** | Mt 26:36 | Mk 14:32 | Lk 22:39-40 | Jn 18:1
- **Request for Peter, James, John to Remain** | Mt 26:36-38 | Mk 14:32-34 | Lk 22:39-40
- **Jesus' Three Prayers in Gethsemane** | Mt 26:39-42 | Mk 14:35-41 | Lk 22:41-44
- **First Return to Peter, James, John Asleep** | Mt 26:40-41 | Mk 14:37
- **Second Return to Peter, James, John Asleep** | Mt 26:43-44 | Mk 14:40
- **Appearance, Strength from Angel** | Lk 22:43
- **Jesus' Sweat like Blood** | Lk 22:44
- **Third Return to Peter, James, John Asleep** | Mt 26:45-46 | Mk 14:41-42 | Lk 22:45-46
- **Judas Betrays Jesus with a Kiss, Soldiers** | Mt 26:47-50 | Mk 14:43-45 | Lk 22:47-48 | Jn 18:2-12
- **Jesus' I AM, Toppling of Authorities, Soldiers** | Jn 18:4-6
- **Jesus Seized by Authorities, Soldiers** | Mt 26:50 | Mk 14:46
- **Peter Attacks, Jesus Heals Malchus** | Mt 26:51-54 | Mk 14:47 | Lk 22:49-51 | Jn 18:10
- **Jesus Rebukes Peter** | Mt 26:52-54 | Jn 18:11
- **Jesus Rebukes the Authorities, Soldiers** | Mt 26:55-56 | Mk 14:48-49 | Lk 22:52-53 | Jn 18:7-9
- **Jesus Abandoned** | Mt 26:56 | Mk 14:50-52
- **Disciple Flees, Loses Garments** | Mk 14:51-52
- **Jesus Taken Away** | Lk 22:54 | Jn 18:12

Climate & Seasonal Context

As Jesus led his disciples into Gethsemane, the weight of the moment was crushing. Though spring days in Jerusalem were mild (~60–75°F), nighttime in the olive grove could drop to 45–55°F, adding to the intensity of what was about to unfold. But the chill in the air was nothing compared to the storm about to break. This was the last moment before the decisive battle—one fought not with swords, but with surrender.

Social, Religious & Political Context

A high-stakes betrayal was underway. The Sanhedrin had convened a secret, illegal trial, proving their desperation to silence Jesus before Passover began. This was more than an arrest—it was a purge. Jesus had disrupted too much, and both the Temple leadership and Rome knew his movement had to be stopped before it spiraled into revolution. His fate had been sealed before he even left the Upper Room.

Yet Jesus' last battle was not against Rome, but against his own flesh. At Gethsemane, he withdrew with Peter, James, and John—the same three who had witnessed his transfiguration and greatest miracles. Now, they saw his agony. Three times, he prayed that the cup of suffering might pass (Matthew 26:39-42), but each time he submitted further. He was no reluctant victim. He was a warrior stepping into his final confrontation. This war was not against an empire but against Sin and Death themselves.

Tactical Insight

Ancient kings and gods often "slept" before a great battle—a final moment of withdrawal before stepping forward to engage Chaos— much like Jesus had slept in the boat before his first battle against the Sea (Matthew 8:18, 23-27). But here, Jesus was the only one awake. His disciples, exhausted and unaware, slept through the most critical moment of their leader's life. Three times he found them unprepared, mirroring the three times Peter would soon deny him.

Then came Judas' betrayal and the power of "I AM." Just as Jesus rose from prayer, Judas arrived with a cohort of soldiers and Temple guards (John 18:2-3). His betrayal was personal, marked by a kiss— the very sign of a disciple's loyalty. But when the guards moved in, Jesus didn't cower. He stepped forward and declared, "I AM" (John 18:4-6). The sheer force of those words—echoing the divine name in Exodus—sent the soldiers falling to the ground. Jesus had just demonstrated his complete authority, yet he let them take him anyway. This moment was not out of his control. He surrendered, not because he was overpowered, but because he had chosen this path.

Still thinking in earthly terms, Peter lashed out, slicing off the ear of Malchus, the high priest's servant (John 18:10). But Jesus immediately rebuked him (Matthew 26:52-54). He could have called down legions of angels, but this was not that kind of war. His path to victory was not through violence, but through surrender. As the guards dragged Jesus away, his disciples scattered into the night (Mark 14:50-52). The ones who had sworn loyalty, who had pledged to die for him, all fled.

Strategic Questions

1. Why didn't Jesus resist? His Empire was not of this world. He was proving that true power comes through self-sacrifice, not force. Every earthly kingdom had been built on conquest, violence, and dominance. But Jesus' movement was founded on an entirely different principle: self-giving love. By refusing to fight back, he was exposing the corruption of the world's power structures. His arrest was not defeat. It was the very act that would establish his Empire forever.

2. Why did he allow Judas to betray him? This betrayal was not an accident but the necessary trigger for the next phase of his mission. Jesus had long predicted his betrayal, but he never tried to prevent it. Without it, there would be no trial, no crucifixion, no resurrection. More than that, Judas' actions revealed a stark contrast in discipleship: he wanted Jesus to seize power by force, but Jesus willingly walked the path of suffering. Judas tried to control the Messiah, while Jesus surrendered to God's plan.

3. What was the significance of "I AM"? By declaring this name, Jesus openly identified himself with God—a final revelation before his execution. When the soldiers came, he did not hide or flee. Instead, he stepped forward and uttered the divine name, the same one God had spoken to Moses at the burning bush (Exodus 3:14). The response was immediate—the soldiers collapsed. This was no normal reaction; this was a supernatural event. In that moment, Jesus made it clear that he was not being taken—he was going willingly. He could have stopped everything with a single word, but instead, he walked forward, knowing that the real battle was about to begin.

4. Why did Peter's sword strike fail? Because the real battle wasn't with Rome or the Sanhedrin—it was against Sin and Death, and they could not be defeated by a blade. When Peter attacked, Jesus stopped him. "Do you think I cannot call on my Father, and he will at once put at my disposal more than twelve legions of angels?" (Matthew 26:52-53). Peter saw the conflict in earthly terms—Jesus vs. the religious leaders, Jesus vs. Rome. But Jesus saw the deeper war. The entire human race was enslaved to Sin and bound to Death. No military uprising, no rebellion could fix this. On the contrary, earthly means of violence toward each other only fed into the goals and desires of Sin and Death. If Jesus had fought Rome like Peter expected, even if he had won, nothing would have truly changed. The world would still be trapped in the same endless cycle of oppression and violence. Jesus'

mission was not to temporarily overthrow an empire—it was to break the power of Sin and Death themselves. To do that, he had to take it upon himself, absorb its full weight, suffer its consequences, and defeat it from within. The sword was useless in this battle. Only the cross could win. Peter's failure symbolized the failure of all human attempts to bring about God's rule through force. The only weapon that could conquer Sin and Death was self-sacrificial love—the weapon Jesus was about to wield.

—SCENE 25—
THE UNJUST TRIBUNAL

Jesus' Trial | Annas' Courtyard, Caiaphas' House, Sanhedrin, Praetorium | Spring 29 AD

Campaign Chronology

- **First Jewish Phase—Annas, Peter's Denial |** Jn 18:13-23
- **Second Jewish Phase—Caiaphas, Sanhedrin |** Mt 26:57-68 | Mk 14:53-65 | Lk 22:54-65 | Jn 18:24
- **Peter's Second, Third Denials |** Mt 26:58-75 | Mk 14:54-72 | Lk 22:54-62 | Jn 18:15-27
- **Third Jewish Phase—Sanhedrin |** Mt 27:1 | Mk 15:1 | Lk 22:66-71
- **Judas' Remorse, Suicide |** Mt 27:3-10 | *Acts 1:18-19*
- **First Roman Phase—Pilate |** Mt 27:2-14 | Mk 15:1-5 | Lk 23:1-5 | Jn 18:28-38
- **Second Roman Phase—Herod Antipas |** Lk 23:6-12
- **Third Roman Phase—Pilate |** Mt 27:15-26 | Mk 15:6-15 | Lk 23:13-25 | Jn 18:39-19:16

Social, Religious & Political Context

Jesus was dragged from Gethsemane to Annas' courtyard, where the first phase of his trial began under the cover of darkness. This was already illegal by Jewish law, as trials were not to be held at night. But the religious leaders weren't concerned with justice. They wanted him condemned before dawn so they could take him to the Roman governor with an already settled verdict.

Annas, the former high priest and godfather of the Temple economy, questioned Jesus (John 18:13-23). But it was clear that this was not a trial—it was an interrogation. The charges weren't even fully formed. They just needed something—anything—to justify what they were about to do.

From Annas' courtyard, Jesus was shuffled to Caiaphas' house, where the Sanhedrin had assembled in violation of their own laws. False witnesses were brought forward, but their testimonies didn't align (Mark 14:55-56). The trial was falling apart—until Caiaphas himself forced the issue.

When pressed, Jesus finally spoke, quoting Daniel 7:13-14—"You will see the Son of Man seated at the right hand of power and coming on the clouds of heaven" (Matthew 26:64). This was an open declaration of divine authority, and Caiaphas tore his robes in outrage. This was the turning point, as they now had their charge: blasphemy. But there was a problem—blasphemy wasn't a capital offense under Roman law. The Sanhedrin had condemned him, but they still needed Pilate's approval for execution.

Peter's denials signaled that the Empire's future might be in jeopardy. As Jesus was interrogated, Peter was outside, crumbling under pressure. Three times he denied knowing Jesus, just as Jesus had predicted. At the moment of Jesus' greatest need, his closest follower abandoned him. But this wasn't just about Peter—it symbolized the entire movement's apparent collapse. Their leader was arrested, their strongest disciple failed, and all seemed lost.

At dawn, Jesus was bound and dragged to Pilate's headquarters. But because Rome didn't care about blasphemy, the Jewish leaders had to frame this as a political crime. So they shifted the charge: Jesus was claiming to be a king—a direct challenge to Caesar (Luke 23:2). Now Pilate had to listen. But when Pilate questioned Jesus, he found no fault in him (John 18:38). This was clearly a manufactured case. Jesus wasn't leading an armed rebellion, and Pilate knew it.

Pilate, not wanting to deal with the mess, sent Jesus to Herod Antipas, the puppet ruler of Galilee, who was also in town for Passover. Herod saw Jesus as a curiosity, not a criminal. He wanted a miracle, not a trial (Luke 23:8-9). When Jesus refused to entertain him and engage in this social gameplay, Herod had him mocked and beaten before sending him back to Pilate. Pilate was now stuck. He knew Jesus was innocent, but the crowd was growing restless. He tried one last maneuver: offering to release either Jesus or Barabbas, a violent insurrectionist. But the chief priests had already stirred the crowd, and they demanded Barabbas. The crowd, representative of human nature, wanted a revolutionary, but they preferred the violent one over the peaceful one. And Pilate gave them what they wanted.

Tactical Insight

Jesus' silence was a blatant challenge to both Rome and the Sanhedrin. As the accusations mounted, Jesus remained silent (Matthew 27:14).

This was not weakness—it was strategy. He was exposing the corruption of the trial, the cowardice of the leaders, and the emptiness of the charges without saying a word. Isaiah 53:7 had prophesied this moment: "Like a lamb led to the slaughter, he did not open his mouth." Jesus was choosing the cross. He wasn't playing their game. His Empire was built on sacrifice, not survival.

Rome and the Temple had chosen their enemy. The Jewish authorities and the Roman state had allied for one brief moment to eliminate the threat of Jesus. The religious elite saw him as a blasphemer, and Rome saw him as a political threat. But in their effort to destroy him, they had only set the stage for his greatest victory. The true King was about to be enthroned—not on a Roman dais, but on a cross. The trial was over, but the revolution had only just begun.

Strategic Questions

1. Why did Jesus stay silent? His silence was a weapon, exposing corruption, fulfilling prophecy, and reinforcing his mission. In an honor-shame society, verbal battles were won through argument and wit, yet Jesus, who had repeatedly dismantled his opponents' arguments, chose near silence at his trial. This was deliberate. By refusing to engage, he controlled the power dynamic, forcing his accusers into desperation. The more they raged, the more they revealed their own hypocrisy and fear. His silence fulfilled Isaiah 53:7. But beyond prophecy, it was an act of defiance, a refusal to play by the rules of corrupt power. His silence was his final, unanswerable argument, leaving his enemies exposed and powerless.

2. Why did Pilate give in? Though he saw that Jesus did not pose a violent political threat, Pilate feared the political consequences of releasing him. Pilate had a history of violently suppressing dissenters. He had provoked riots with imperial banners in the Temple and clubbed protesters to death. Yet now he hesitated. By this time, he may have been on thin ice with Rome. If another uprising occurred under his watch, it could cost him his position—or worse. The religious leaders exploited this, pressuring him by implying that freeing Jesus would make him an enemy of Caesar (John 19:12). Pilate's decision wasn't about justice but self-preservation. He didn't fear Jesus. He feared appearing weak before Rome.

3. What was the significance of Barabbas? The crowd chose a violent revolutionary over a peaceful one, revealing how deeply they misunderstood Jesus' messianic mission. Barabbas wasn't just a criminal. He was part of an insurrection against Rome. The people had a choice between two messianic figures: one who wielded the sword and one who wielded self-sacrificial love. They chose the sword. They

wanted a leader who would kill for them, not one who would die for them. Their decision reflected their longing for a military messiah like King David or Judas Maccabee. Ironically, by rejecting Jesus, they secured the very victory he came to achieve—his death was the moment his true Empire was established.

4. Why did the Sanhedrin manipulate the charges? They knew Rome wouldn't execute Jesus for religious blasphemy, so they highlighted his political identity. Blasphemy was a capital offense under Jewish law, but not under Roman rule. The Sanhedrin needed to make Jesus appear as a rival to Caesar, forcing Pilate's hand. Their fear of Jesus wasn't just religious but political and economic. The Temple system controlled Jewish life, from worship to commerce. And Jesus' movement threatened their power, disrupting the Temple economy and exposing corruption. His popularity could destabilize their alliance with Rome. By accusing Jesus of claiming kingship, they turned their own fear of losing power into a charge against him— ironically, securing the very kingdom they sought to prevent.

—SCENE 26—
BATTLE TO THE DEATH

Jesus' Crucifixion & Burial | Praetorium, Golgatha | Spring 29 AD

Campaign Chronology

- **Jesus Mocked by Roman Soldiers |** Mt 27:27-30 | Mk 15:16-19
- **Journey to Golgatha |** Mt 27:31-34 | Mk 15:20-23 | Lk 23:26-33 | Jn 19:16-17
- **First Three Hours of Crucifixion |** Mt 27:35-44 | Mk 15:24-32 | Lk 23:33-43 | Jn 19:18-27
- **Last Three Hours of Crucifixion |** Mt 27:45-50 | Mk 15:33-37 | Lk 23:44-46 | Jn 19:28-30
- **Jesus' Death |** Mt 27:51-56 | Mk 15:38-41 | Lk 23:45-49
- **Jesus Declared Dead on Cross, Removed |** Mt 27:57-58 | Mk 15:42-45 | Lk 23:50-52 | Jn 19:31-38
- **Jesus Placed in Tomb |** Mt 27:59-60 | Mk 15:46 | Lk 23:53-54 | Jn 19:39-42
- **Soldiers Guard, Women Watch Tomb |** Mt 27:61-66 | Mk 15:47 | Lk 23:55-56

Social, Religious & Political Context

The cross was a Roman statement of political power. Crucifixion wasn't just execution—it was a public, calculated act of dominance.

Rome reserved it for insurrectionists, ensuring their deaths were not only agonizing but also public warnings against rebellion. Victims were stripped, beaten, and left to die slowly, their suffering a grotesque spectacle meant to reinforce Rome's absolute control. Jesus wasn't just being killed. He was being erased. The mockery, the flogging, the crown of thorns—all of it was designed to crush his claim to kingship, to turn him into a joke before he died. But something else was happening. The cross, meant to display Roman power, was becoming the throne of the true King. What was meant to humiliate Jesus was instead revealing his glorious authority.

After his brutal flogging, Jesus was forced to carry the horizontal beam of his cross through the crowded streets of Jerusalem. This was not just punishment. It was Rome's perverse version of a death march—a final display of control before execution.

At Golgotha, Jesus was nailed to the cross between two insurrectionists, fulfilling Isaiah's prophecy that he would be "numbered with rebels" (Isaiah 53:12). Above him, a sign read, "Jesus of Nazareth, King of the Jews" (John 19:19). Pilate had it written in multiple languages—Hebrew, Latin, and Greek—so that all who passed by could read it. It was meant as irony. But, in reality, it was the greatest proclamation of truth.

At noon, the sky went dark (Mark 15:33). This was no ordinary eclipse. This was a sign of cosmic mourning, a shadow over creation itself as the King was being slain. At about 3:00 p.m., Jesus cried out in Aramaic, *Eli, Eli, lama sabachthani?*—"My God, my God, why have you forsaken me?" (Matthew 27:46). These were words of despair taken from the opening line of Psalm 22, which begins in agony but ends in victory. Even in his suffering and utter dejection, he was declaring the certainty of his triumph. Then, with his final breath, Jesus proclaimed, "It is finished" (John 19:30). Not that "he" was finished, but his mission. The battle was won.

Then the earth shook, the rocks split, and the tombs were opened (Matthew 27:51-52). This was no ordinary earthquake—it was Death itself rupturing under the weight of Jesus' victory. Just as Lazarus' resurrection (John 11) had been the first major strike against Death, Matthew envisioned Death as the ancient Canaanite and Israelite devourer, being forced to regurgitate its prey. In ancient myth, Death swallowed victims whole, his insatiable maw never filled. Yet here he is made to vomit out the dead, unable to hold them in the wake of Jesus' sacrifice. For, the old cosmic order held that a life reclaimed meant a life owed. Jesus had willingly become the offering, paying with his own life to break Death's hold—not just for Lazarus, but for all those who had been swallowed by the grave. The tombs that had consumed were made to release. This would foreshadow the final battle to come, when, in full, "Death will be swallowed up in victory" (Isaiah 25:8, 1 Corinthians 15:54). The cross, meant to seal Jesus' defeat, instead became the catalyst for Death's undoing.

The paradox of the cross was that defeat was the way to true, lasting victory. To Rome, this was just another execution. Another failed revolutionary put down before his movement could take root. But in reality, this was the moment of enthronement. The cross, meant to display Rome's strength, had instead become the place of divine victory. Jesus' death was not the end. It was the beginning of the true Empire. The only question was: Did Rome, the Temple authorities, and Death itself have any idea what was about to happen next?

Strategic Questions

1. Why was crucifixion significant? It was Rome's method for executing insurrectionists, making Jesus' death a direct challenge to Caesar's rule. But instead of proving Rome's power, the cross became the means of his enthronement.

2. Why did Jesus refuse to fight back? His Empire was built on sacrificial love, not violent resistance. By absorbing Rome's violence, he exposed its corruption and revealed true kingship.

3. Why did darkness cover the land? It was a cosmic sign that something beyond human politics was taking place. Heaven and earth were bearing witness to the death of the Son of God.

4. Why did the centurion recognize him? The first person to declare Jesus as the Son of God at his death was not a disciple, not a priest, not a Jewish leader—but a Roman soldier. The old world order was already crumbling.

—SCENE 27—
THE ULTIMATE VICTORY

Jesus' Resurrection | Golgatha, Bethany, Jerusalem | Spring 29 AD

Campaign Chronology

- **Women Visit Jesus' Tomb |** Mt 28:1 | Mk 16:1
- **Stone Rolled Away |** Mt 28:2-4
- **Women Find Tomb Empty |** Mt 28:5-8 | Mk 16:2-8 | Lk 24:1-8 | Jn 20:1
- **Peter, John Find Tomb Empty |** Lk 24:9-12 | Jn 20:2-10

Climate & Seasonal Context

Spring in Jerusalem meant mild temperatures, typically ranging from 60–75°F, making travel and public gatherings easier. With Passover just ending, many pilgrims were still in the city, ensuring that whatever happened next would spread quickly. The early mornings, however, remained cool, adding to the eerie stillness when the first witnesses arrived at the tomb.

Geographical Insight

The events of the resurrection took place in and around Jerusalem. Golgotha, the execution site, was just outside the city walls, ensuring public visibility. Roman crucifixions were meant to be seen as a deterrent. The burial took place in a rock-cut tomb, a type of grave used by wealthier Jewish families. Joseph of Arimathea, a respected Sanhedrin member, had provided the tomb, unknowingly fulfilling Isaiah's prophecy that the Messiah would be "with a rich man in his death" (Isaiah 53:9). Jesus' post-resurrection appearances were centered in Jerusalem, the epicenter of both religious and political power, as well as Bethany, where he had often retreated in the final days of his ministry.

Social, Religious & Political Context

Fearing that Jesus' followers might steal the body and claim he had risen, the Jewish leaders pressured Pilate to secure the tomb. Roman guards were stationed there, and an official seal was placed on the entrance—a seal that, under Roman law, no one could break without facing severe punishment. This was an effort to control the narrative. If Jesus' body remained in the tomb, his movement would die with him. If it disappeared, authorities could claim fraud. But their own attempt to prevent deception would become proof of the resurrection.

Tactical Insight

Early in the morning, a group of women approached the tomb, expecting to anoint a lifeless body. Instead, they found the stone rolled away and the guards collapsed in fear. The tomb was empty. A messenger delivered the words that would change history: "Why do you seek the living among the dead? He is not here—he has risen!" (Luke 24:5-6). This was not just a personal miracle. It was a direct challenge to every power that had sought to silence Jesus. Rome had executed him. The Temple authorities had condemned him. Death had claimed him. And yet, none of them could hold him.

The first witnesses of the resurrection were women—an astonishing detail in a time when female testimony was not legally valid. If the story had been fabricated, the authors would have certainly chosen male witnesses to give it credibility. Instead, Mary Magdalene and the other women were the ones entrusted with announcing the news. This was not accidental. Jesus had already elevated women throughout his ministry, and now they were the first messengers of the risen King. Their testimony, though weak in human courts, was unshakable in the eyes of God.

The Jewish leaders, upon hearing that the body was gone, scrambled to cover up the event. The Roman guards were bribed to spread the story that Jesus' disciples had stolen the body. Yet this explanation made little sense. The disciples had scattered in fear at his arrest. Were they now capable of overpowering trained soldiers? If the authorities had possession of the body, why not display it and crush the movement immediately? Their very efforts to suppress the resurrection only made it more undeniable.

Unlike visions or symbolic resurrections found in mythology, Jesus' appearances after rising from the dead were physical and tangible. He spoke with his followers, ate with them, and invited them to touch his wounds. Peter and John ran to the tomb and found the burial cloths still there, but no body. Mary Magdalene saw him first in the garden, mistaking him for the gardener until he spoke her name. Two disciples walked with him on the road to Emmaus, recognizing him only when he broke bread. The Eleven saw him together in the upper room, where he proved he was not a ghost by eating in their presence. These were not fleeting visions but real, bodily encounters that changed everything.

Strategic Questions

1. Why was the tomb guarded? The Jewish leaders feared that the movement would continue, but their attempt to prevent deception only confirmed the truth of the resurrection.

2. Why did Jesus appear to women first? His Empire redefined power—not by status, but by faith. Those considered weak by society were entrusted with the greatest news in history.

3. Why didn't Jesus appear to the authorities? His kingdom was not built on proving himself to corrupt leaders. Instead, he appeared to those who would carry the message forward.

4. Why was the tomb empty instead of just visions of Jesus? If the resurrection had been only spiritual, the authorities could simply have displayed the body. But they couldn't because it was gone. The resurrection was not just the vindication of Jesus' mission. It was the

moment Death itself was defeated. Every force that had tried to stop him had failed. The authorities thought they had silenced him, but in reality, his Empire had just begun.

—SCENE 28—
The KING'S VICTORY TOUR

Resurrection Appearances, Ascension | Golgatha, Jerusalem, Emmaus Road, Galilee | Spring 29 AD

Campaign Chronology

- **Jesus Appears to Mary Magdalene** | Mk 16:9-11 | Jn 20:11-18
- **Jesus Appears to Other Women** | Mt 28:9-10
- **Soldiers Report to Jewish Authorities** | Mt 28:11-15
- **Two Men See Jesus on Way to Emmaus** | Mk 16:12-13 | Lk 24:13-32
- **Two Men Report to Rest of Disciples** | Lk 24:33-35 | *1 Cor 15:5*
- **Jesus Appears to Group of Ten** | Mk 16:14 | Lk 24:36-43 | Jn 20:19-25
- **Jesus Appears to Group of Eleven** | Jn 20:26-31 | *1 Cor 15:5*
- **Jesus Appears to Seven at Sea of Galilee** | Jn 21:1-25
- **Jesus Appears to Eleven (+) on Mountain** | Mt 28:16-20 | Mk 16:15-18 | *1 Cor 15:6*
- **Jesus Appears to Jacob (James)** | *1 Cor 15:7*
- **Jesus Appears to Disciples in Jerusalem** | Lk 24:44-49 | *Acts 1:3-8*
- **Jesus Ascends from Mount of Olives** | Mk 16:19-20 | Lk 24:50-53 | *Acts 1:9-12*

Climate & Seasonal Context

With Passover just ending, many pilgrims remained in and around Jerusalem, ensuring that reports of Jesus' resurrection would spread quickly. The mild spring weather made travel between cities more manageable, allowing his followers to regroup and prepare for their next steps.

Geographical Insight

Jesus' post-resurrection appearances took place in key locations tied to his mission. Jerusalem remained the epicenter of religious authority and Roman control, where his presence was most politically charged. The road to Emmaus, a small town west of Jerusalem, became a symbolic setting for revealing his true mission. Galilee, where it had all begun, served as the base for final preparations before the movement expanded beyond Israel. Finally, the Mount of Olives, the prophesied location of the Messiah's triumph (Zechariah 14:4), became the site of his ascension.

Social, Religious & Political Context

The resurrection wasn't just a spiritual event. It was a direct challenge to both Rome and the Jewish authorities. Jesus' death was supposed to end his movement, but now his followers were claiming he had risen. The authorities had no explanation for the empty tomb, and despite their efforts to suppress the news, the story was spreading. The disciples, once scattered in fear, were now gathering again, preparing for something bigger.

Tactical Insight

On the road to Emmaus, two disciples left Jerusalem, believing all hope was lost. Jesus joined them, unrecognized, and walked with them as they expressed their confusion. Instead of revealing himself immediately, he explained how his death and resurrection fulfilled the Hebrew Scriptures. Only when he broke bread did they recognize him (Luke 24:13-35). This moment redefined their expectations. Jesus had conquered, but not through military force. His Empire was not of this world's order.

Before ascending, Jesus led his followers back to Galilee (Matthew 28:16). This was a crucial strategic move. Galilee had been the movement's stronghold, far from the immediate threats of Jerusalem. Returning there allowed him to reinforce the mission, reassure his disciples, and prepare them for their global expansion. It was there that he gave them their final orders—the so-called Great Commission.

On a mountain in Galilee, Jesus declared his universal rule (Matthew 28:18-20).

- "All authority in heaven and on earth has been given to me." The resurrection was not just personal vindication—it was a declaration of kingship over all creation.
- "Go and make disciples of all nations." His mission was no longer confined to Israel—this was now a worldwide movement.
- "Baptizing them… teaching them… I am with you always." His Empire would expand not by conquest, but by transformation.

This was a direct challenge to Rome's power. Caesar claimed dominion over the earth, but Jesus now declared absolute authority over heaven and earth.

The final act took place on the Mount of Olives (Acts 1:9-12), a location loaded with messianic significance. Instead of launching an earthly revolt, Jesus ascended into the heavens, fulfilling the vision of Daniel 7:13-14, where the Son of Man is given dominion over all nations. His departure was not an end. It was just the beginning.

Strategic Questions

1. Why return to Galilee before ascending? To regroup his followers, reinforce the mission, and prepare them for global expansion. Jesus grew his movement in Galilee, and most of his early followers were Galileans. But most of them probably did not witness the final events in Jerusalem, nor did they see his crucifixion firsthand. Having heard about it, they would have been devastated, even if they had also heard about Jesus' resurrection. Seeing Jesus face-to-face in the wake of these monumental events confirmed their ideas about him as the Messiah and reassured them that he was the Son of God.

2. Why reveal himself gradually and selectively? For a couple of reasons. To allow his movement time to develop. Had Jesus come out at the beginning and declared publicly and demonstratively, "I am the Messiah and Son of God!" he would have been stopped before his movement began. However, he wanted not only to defeat Death by submitting himself to it, but he also wanted to launch a movement that would change the world here and now. This could only happen if he gave it time to develop and grow, and in that time show how he wanted his newly established Empire to operate.

3. Why not stay on earth to rule? His Empire was never meant to be confined to one place. His reign would be carried out through his Spirit and his followers. The Book of Acts recalls the way this unfolded among Jesus' earliest followers, and other New Testament works unpack the theological and practical aspects of his life and movement.

4. Why ascend in front of witnesses? To mark the transfer of authority and confirm his role as the true ruler of heaven and earth. The global mission had begun, as the King had won. The old order had been overthrown. But the war was not over. Now, his followers were called to spread the victory to every nation. The resurrection wasn't just about Jesus—it was the launch of a revolution that would reshape the world.

SECTION III—ADDITIONAL MATERIAL

—ABOUT THE GOSPELS & THE LIFE OF JESUS—
DATES, SOURCES & LANGUAGES

In this section, we explore the historical foundations of the Gospels, including their dating, manuscript evidence, and the languages spoken in Jesus' time. Rather than late, unreliable compositions, the Gospels are among the most well-preserved and widely attested ancient texts, with thousands of manuscript sources and early citations confirming their authenticity. We also examine the linguistic landscape of first-century Judea, emphasizing Jesus' primary language—Galilean Aramaic—alongside the Greek, Hebrew, and Latin influences present in his world. This section provides a solid historical and textual foundation for understanding the life and mission of Jesus as recorded in the Gospels.

THE DATE OF JESUS' BIRTH & PUBLIC CAMPAIGN

The question of when Jesus was born and when his public campaign began has been the subject of significant scholarly debate. While no single piece of evidence provides a definitive date, a synthesis of historical records, early Christian tradition, and astronomical data allows for a strong argument that Jesus was born in 3/2 BC and began his public campaign, alongside John the Baptist, in 26/27 AD.

Determining Jesus' birth year requires careful consideration of the reign of Herod the Great, since the Gospel of Matthew (2:1) states that Jesus was born during Herod's lifetime. The traditional dating of Herod's death to 4 BC has often led scholars to propose a birth date for Jesus around 6–4 BC, but a closer look at Josephus' account suggests an alternative timeline. Josephus states that Herod died after a lunar eclipse and before Passover (Antiquities 17.6.4). While a partial lunar eclipse did occur in March 4 BC, a more significant eclipse took place on January 10, 1 BC, allowing for a better fit with Josephus' timeline of events between the eclipse and Passover. If Herod died in 1 BC, then Jesus' birth would naturally shift to a later date—most likely 3 or 2 BC.

Additional support for this timeframe comes from Roman historical records and early Christian sources. Luke's Gospel (2:1–2) places Jesus' birth during a census associated with Quirinius, governor of Syria. While Quirinius is known to have conducted a census in 6 AD, Tertullian and other early Christian writers suggest that an earlier registration under Augustus in 3/2 BC may have been the one Luke referenced. This coincided with the emperor's empire-wide loyalty oath upon receiving the title "Father of the Fatherland," which may explain why Joseph and Mary had to return to Bethlehem.

Astronomical data also aligns with this period. The Star of Bethlehem, described in Matthew 2:2, has been linked to notable celestial events in 3/2 BC, including a triple conjunction of Jupiter and Regulus and a rare Jupiter-Venus conjunction, which would have been seen as an important sign by Eastern astrologers. Early Christian sources further reinforce this dating—Clement of Alexandria, Irenaeus, and Eusebius all place Jesus' birth within this general timeframe, with Clement specifically dating it to the 28th year of Augustus, corresponding to 2 BC.

If Jesus was born in 3/2 BC, the start of his public campaign should be placed approximately thirty years later, in line with Luke 3:23. Luke also provides a more specific historical marker: John the Baptist began preaching in the fifteenth year of Tiberius Caesar (Luke 3:1–2). Since Tiberius' reign can be counted either from his co-regency with Augustus in 11/12 AD or Augustus' death in 14 AD, his fifteenth year falls in either 26 or 29 AD. The former date (26/27 AD) aligns well with other historical indicators and fits within the timeframe of Pontius Pilate's governorship (26–36 AD), allowing for just over a two-year campaign leading to Jesus' crucifixion in 29 AD.

Further confirmation comes from John 2:20, where Jewish leaders tell Jesus that the Temple had been under construction for 46 years. Since Herod the Great began major renovations in 20/19 BC, this conversation must have taken place around 27 AD, placing Jesus' campaign within the correct window. Additionally, John the Baptist, who was about six months older than Jesus (Luke 1:26–36), likely began his public campaign slightly earlier in 26 AD, preparing the way for Jesus to emerge publicly in 27 AD.

By bringing together historical records, biblical chronology, and early Christian tradition, we can construct a coherent timeline for Jesus' life and campaign:

- **3/2 BC**—Jesus is born in Bethlehem, during the reign of Herod the Great.
- **1 BC**—Herod dies, eliminating the need for a 4 BC birthdate.
- **26 AD**—John the Baptist begins preaching, calling for repentance.
- **27 AD**—Jesus begins his public campaign after his baptism and time in the wilderness.
- **29 AD**—Jesus is crucified under Pontius Pilate.

This chronology harmonizes the best available historical and biblical evidence, making a 3/2 BC birth and a 26/27 AD public campaign the most compelling and well-supported reconstruction of Jesus' timeline.

THE DATING, PROVENANCE & RELIABILITY OF THE GOSPELS

The four canonical Gospels—Matthew, Mark, Luke, and John—stand as the primary sources for the life and campaign of Jesus. While modern scholarship offers a range of theories regarding their dating, authorship, and reliability, a more traditional and historically grounded approach affirms that these texts were written by the apostles and their close associates within the first century, preserving eyewitness testimony and early Christian tradition.

Dating and Authorship

Mark, the earliest Gospel, is traditionally attributed to John Mark, a companion of Peter (1 Pet. 5:13). Early Christian sources such as Papias (c. 125 AD) affirm that Mark recorded Peter's preaching, which explains its vivid, fast-paced narrative. Conservative dating places it around 50–60 AD, possibly during Peter's advancement of the Jesus Movement in Rome.

Matthew, written by the apostle Matthew (Levi), was likely composed in the 50s or 60s AD. Early church tradition states that Matthew originally wrote in Hebrew or Aramaic, later translating or adapting it into Greek. The Gospel's strong Jewish focus—frequent Old Testament citations and concern for Jesus' fulfillment of prophecy—suggests an audience of Jewish Christians, possibly in Antioch or Jerusalem.

Luke, authored by Luke the physician, a companion of Paul (Col. 4:14), is part of a two-volume work with Acts. Luke's Gospel is carefully researched (Luke 1:1–4), based on eyewitness testimony. Dating aligns with 60–62 AD, as Acts ends before Paul's execution, suggesting the Gospel was completed before 64 AD, during Paul's Roman imprisonment.

John, the last Gospel, is attributed to John the apostle. Internal evidence (John 21:24) and early church testimony confirm this. Likely written between 80–90 AD, John's Gospel complements the Synoptics with a theological focus on Jesus' divine identity. John's strong Palestinian Jewish perspective, combined with its developed Christology, suggests it was written for both Jewish and Gentile believers, possibly in Ephesus.

Provenance and Reliability

The Gospels were written within living memory of the events they describe. They reflect deep familiarity with first-century Jewish customs, geography, and political structures, which would be difficult to fabricate. Moreover, the Gospels' authors wrote in an oral culture where memorization and communal storytelling ensured fidelity to original events. While critics often emphasize variations between the Gospels, such differences align with ancient biographical writing rather than errors. The core message remains consistent, reinforcing their reliability.

The historical reliability of the Gospels is unparalleled when compared to other ancient texts. There are over 5,800 Greek manuscripts of the New Testament, with thousands more in Latin, Coptic, Syriac, and other early translations. Some of the earliest fragments, such as P52 (a portion of John's Gospel), date to around 125 AD, within a generation of the original writing. In contrast, major works of antiquity—such as Tacitus' Annals (written c. 100 AD, earliest manuscript from 9th–11th century AD) and Plato's dialogues (written 4th century BC, earliest manuscript from 9th century AD)— have far fewer manuscripts and significantly later copies. Even the widely accepted accounts of Julius Caesar's Gallic Wars (written c. 50s BC) rest on just ten surviving manuscripts, the earliest from 900 years after Caesar's time. Despite this, scholars generally trust these works as accurate historical accounts. Given the Gospels' far superior manuscript evidence, their early dating, and their preservation in diverse textual traditions, they stand among the best-attested documents of antiquity.

Additionally, skeptics often claim that the Gospels were written "hundreds of years after Jesus," yet the overwhelming manuscript evidence contradicts this. The four Gospels were all completed within the first century AD, well within the lifespan of eyewitnesses. Church fathers such as Irenaeus (c. 180 AD) and Papias (c. 125 AD) directly reference the Gospels, confirming their early use. This is in stark contrast to Alexander the Great, whose most detailed biographies— by Arrian and Plutarch—were written over 400 years after his death (323 BC), yet historians widely accept them as authoritative. If the standards used against the Gospels were applied to other ancient figures, virtually all of ancient history would be in doubt. The vast manuscript tradition, early citations, and widespread transmission of the Gospels make them not only historically credible but among the best-preserved texts from antiquity.

The Gospels present historically credible, eyewitness-based testimony, rooted in early Christian communities that preserved and transmitted Jesus' words and deeds. When considered alongside external sources like Josephus, Tacitus, and early church fathers, they provide a compelling, well-grounded account of Jesus' life and campaign, and the emergence of the Christian movement.

THE LANGUAGES OF JESUS & HIS WORLD

Jesus lived in first-century Galilee, a multilingual region influenced by Aramaic, Hebrew, Greek, and Latin. The question of which languages he spoke is crucial for understanding his teachings and interactions with various groups. While Aramaic was his primary language, he likely had familiarity with Hebrew and Greek, and possibly some Latin in limited contexts.

Jesus' Primary Language: Galilean Aramaic

- Aramaic was the dominant spoken language in Galilee and Judea, used in daily life.
- Jesus' sayings preserved in Aramaic include expressions like *Talitha koum* ("Little girl, arise," Mark 5:41) and *Eloi, Eloi, lama sabachthani* ("My God, My God, why have you forsaken me?" Mark 15:34).
- The Galilean dialect of Aramaic differed from that of Judea, possibly explaining why Peter's speech was recognizable in Jerusalem (Matt. 26:73).

Hebrew: The Language of Scripture and Worship

- Hebrew was used primarily in religious settings—in synagogue readings and Temple rituals.
- Jesus frequently cited the Hebrew Scriptures, as seen in his debates with Pharisees (Matt. 22:41–46) and in his reading from Isaiah in the Nazareth synagogue (Luke 4:16–21).

Greek: The Language of Commerce and Governance

- Greek was the lingua franca of the eastern Roman Empire and commonly spoken in cities.
- Jesus interacted with Greek-speaking Gentiles (e.g., the Syrophoenician woman in Mark 7:26).
- Some of his conversations, such as with Pontius Pilate (John 18:33–38), may have taken place in Greek.

Latin: The Language of Roman Administration

- Latin was less common but used by Roman authorities.
- Pilate's inscription on the cross was written in Latin, Greek, and Hebrew (John 19:20), indicating Jesus' execution had to be understood by a diverse audience.
- It is unlikely that Jesus spoke much Latin, but he may have understood basic terms from Roman officials.

Jesus primarily spoke Galilean Aramaic, but he also had competency in Hebrew and Greek. His multilingual ability allowed him to communicate with Jewish, Samaritan, and Gentile audiences, shaping his interactions and teachings.

In this section, you'll find short descriptions of the important people and places in Jesus' world. From religious sects like the Pharisees and Sadducees to political groups like the Romans and Herodians, these entries provide insight into the figures who shaped the events of the Gospels. You'll also discover key locations—from bustling cities like Jerusalem and Capernaum to the wilderness retreats that played a role in Jesus' campaign. These descriptions are designed to help you better understand the historical, cultural, and geographical context of the Gospels and how each of these individuals and places contributed to the unfolding of Jesus' mission.

PEOPLE IN JESUS' WORLD

Essenes: The Wilderness Ascetics. The Essenes were an apocalyptic Jewish sect that separated from the Temple establishment, believing it had become corrupt. They lived in monastic-like communities, the most famous being at Qumran, near the Dead Sea. Their writings, the Dead Sea Scrolls, emphasize a coming Messianic age, purification rituals, and divine judgment.

John the Baptist's lifestyle—his wilderness preaching, focus on repentance, and use of Isaiah 40:3–5—suggests influence from the Essenes. Jesus, too, shares certain themes with the Essenes, such as the idea of a New Covenant (Luke 22:20, cf. the Dead Sea Scrolls' Damascus Document) and idea that they were "paving the way of the Lord," serving as the desert forerunners who would preface the physical, glorious arrival of God himself (cf. the Dead Sea Scrolls' Community Rule). However, Jesus' openness to sinners and his non-separatist approach contrast with Essene exclusivity. In Phase 1 of the Chronology, John the Baptist, influenced by this movement, emerges from the wilderness calling for repentance in preparation for the coming Kingdom.

Herodians: The Political Loyalists. The Herodians were not a religious sect but a political faction that supported the rule of Herod Antipas and his dynasty, which was installed by Rome. They were allies of the Sadducees and Roman authorities, seeing Jesus as a destabilizing force who could disrupt the fragile balance between Jewish rule and Roman oversight.

In the Gospels, the Herodians appear alongside the Pharisees as part of a conspiracy to trap Jesus (Mark 3:6, 12:13). They were particularly interested in his stance on paying taxes to Caesar (Mark

12:13–17), a key political issue. In Phase 5 of the Chronology, the Herodians, along with the chief priests and Pharisees, intensify their efforts to eliminate Jesus, viewing him as a threat to Herod's rule and Roman order.

Pharisees: The Guardians of the Law. The Pharisees were a dominant religious group known for their strict adherence to the Torah and oral traditions. They believed in resurrection, angels, and divine judgment, setting them apart from the Sadducees. They often clashed with Jesus over Sabbath laws (Mark 2:23–3:6), purity regulations (Matthew 15:1–9), and association with sinners (Luke 5:30–32).

Though they opposed Jesus, not all were hostile. Nicodemus, a Pharisee, met with Jesus privately (John 3:1–21), and Joseph of Arimathea, a member of the ruling council, buried Jesus' body (Luke 23:50–53). In Phase 2 of the Chronology, the Pharisees' conflicts with Jesus escalate, leading to their active role in his eventual arrest.

Priests: The Temple Authority. The priesthood, led by the high priest and his family, controlled the Temple in Jerusalem. Most priests were Sadducees, maintaining power through their cooperation with Rome. Their authority came from their role in sacrifices and the maintenance of purity laws.

Jesus frequently clashes with the priests, particularly during Phase 5, when he challenges their corruption in the Temple (Matthew 21:12–17). The high priest, Caiaphas, plays a central role in Jesus' trial, arguing that it is better for one man to die than for the nation to suffer (John 11:49–53). The chief priests (often mentioned in the Gospels) were a group of powerful Sadducean leaders who managed the Temple's daily operations and conspired with the Sanhedrin to have Jesus arrested and executed (Matthew 26:3–4).

Romans: The Imperial Enforcers. Rome controlled Judea through governors like Pontius Pilate, who ruled from 26–36 AD. Roman authority was maintained through military presence, heavy taxation, and local client kings (like Herod Antipas).

While Rome allowed Jewish religious practices, they were intolerant of rebellion. The Roman centurions in the Gospels, however, are sometimes portrayed positively—one in Capernaum has faith in Jesus' healing power (Matthew 8:5–13), and another at the crucifixion declares, "Truly, this man was the Son of God" (Mark 15:39). In Phase 5 of the Chronology, Pilate finds Jesus innocent but ultimately condemns him under pressure from Jewish leaders (John 19:12–16). The Roman soldiers mock, torture, and crucify Jesus, yet his execution subverts Roman power by becoming his moment of enthronement.

Sadducees: The Temple Aristocracy. The Sadducees were a wealthy and influential Jewish sect that controlled the Temple priesthood and rejected beliefs in angels, resurrection, and an afterlife (Acts 23:8). They were closely aligned with Rome, prioritizing political stability and maintaining their own power.

In Phase 5 of the Chronology, the Sadducees, particularly the chief priests, orchestrate Jesus' arrest and trial. They challenge him on the resurrection (Matthew 22:23–33), seeking to undermine his authority. Their power was deeply tied to the Temple system, which Jesus directly confronted during his campaign.

Scribes: The Experts in the Law. Scribes were professional interpreters and teachers of the Torah, often associated with the Pharisees. They were responsible for copying, preserving, and applying Jewish law in daily life. Some were part of the Sanhedrin, the ruling Jewish council.

The Gospels frequently portray scribes as opponents of Jesus, accusing him of blasphemy when he forgives sins (Mark 2:6–7) and challenging his teachings (Matthew 22:35). Jesus rebukes them for placing heavy burdens on people while neglecting mercy (Matthew 23:2–4). In Phase 2 of the Chronology, Jesus' growing popularity leads to increasing opposition from the scribes, who question his authority and seek ways to discredit him.

Tax Collectors: The Hated Collaborators. Tax collectors were among the most despised individuals in Jewish society. They collected taxes for Rome and often overcharged, enriching themselves at the expense of their fellow Jews. They were considered traitors and were often lumped together with sinners (Matthew 9:10–11).

Yet, Jesus dined with tax collectors, offering them inclusion in his Kingdom. Levi (Matthew), one of Jesus' disciples, was a tax collector before his calling (Mark 2:14–17). Zacchaeus, another tax collector, repented and pledged to repay those he had wronged (Luke 19:1–10). In Phase 2 of the Chronology, Jesus' association with tax collectors scandalizes the religious elite, reinforcing that his movement welcomes the outcasts and the disreputable.

Zealots: The Fighters for Jewish Liberation. The formal Zealot movement did not emerge until the Jewish Revolt (66–73 AD), but the seeds of zealous opposition to Rome were present in Jesus' time. Many Jews hoped for a Messiah who would lead a military rebellion against Roman rule, and some engaged in guerrilla resistance.

One of Jesus' disciples, Simon the Zealot (Luke 6:15), may have been associated with such groups. Barabbas, the prisoner released instead of Jesus, was likely a revolutionary (Mark 15:7). Jesus, however, rejected violent resistance, redefining his Kingdom as one not of this world (John 18:36). In Phase 5 of the Chronology, his refusal to lead an armed revolt disappoints many, including possibly Judas Iscariot, contributing to his betrayal.

PLACES IN JESUS' WORLD

Bethany. A small village on the eastern slope of the Mount of Olives, Bethany was the home of Mary, Martha, and Lazarus (John 11:1–44). Jesus often stayed here when visiting Jerusalem and performed the dramatic resurrection of Lazarus here.

Bethlehem. Known as the "City of David," Bethlehem was the prophesied birthplace of the Messiah (Micah 5:2) and where Jesus was born (Matthew 2:1, Luke 2:4–7). Located just south of Jerusalem, it was also the setting for King David's early life.

Bethsaida. A fishing village on the northern shore of the Sea of Galilee, Bethsaida was the hometown of Peter, Andrew, and Philip (John 1:44). Jesus performed several miracles here, including healing a blind man (Mark 8:22–26) and feeding the five thousand nearby (Luke 9:10–17). Despite these miracles, Jesus condemned Bethsaida for its lack of faith (Matthew 11:21, Luke 10:13).

Caesarea Maritima. Built by Herod the Great, this Roman port city served as the administrative capital of Judea. Pontius Pilate governed from here, and it later became significant in early Christianity as the home of Cornelius, the first Gentile convert (Acts 10).

Caesarea Philippi. Located north of Galilee, this Greco-Roman city was known for pagan worship and the cult of Pan. It was here that Peter famously declared Jesus as the Messiah (Matthew 16:13–20), marking a turning point in Jesus' campaign.

Cana. A small village in Galilee where Jesus performed his first public miracle—turning water into wine at a wedding (John 2:1–11).

Capernaum. A major hub for Jesus' campaign, Capernaum was a fishing town on the northwestern shore of the Sea of Galilee. Jesus performed many healings here (Mark 1:21–34), called several disciples (Matthew 4:13–22), and taught in its synagogue (John 6:59).

Chorazin. A town near the Sea of Galilee, Chorazin was one of the places where Jesus performed miracles, yet it largely rejected his message. He pronounced a woe upon it for its unbelief (Matthew 11:21–22, Luke 10:13–14).

Decapolis. A federation of ten Greco-Roman cities east of the Jordan River, Decapolis was largely Gentile in culture. Jesus visited this region and performed miracles, including healing the demon-possessed man in Gerasa (Mark 5:1–20) and healing a deaf-mute (Mark 7:31–37).

Emmaus. A village near Jerusalem where Jesus appeared to two disciples after his resurrection (Luke 24:13–35).

Gennesaret. A fertile plain on the western shore of the Sea of Galilee, known for its agricultural productivity. Jesus landed here after walking on water and performed many healings (Matthew 14:34–36).

Gerasa (or Gadara). A city in the Decapolis, this is where Jesus cast demons into a herd of pigs, which then ran into the sea (Mark 5:1–20, Luke 8:26–39). The event stirred controversy, and the locals asked Jesus to leave the area.

Gethsemane. A garden at the foot of the Mount of Olives where Jesus prayed in agony before his arrest (Matthew 26:36–46, Mark 14:32–42, Luke 22:39–46).

Golgotha (Calvary). Meaning "Place of the Skull," Golgotha was the site of Jesus' crucifixion just outside Jerusalem's city walls (Matthew 27:33, Mark 15:22, John 19:17).

Hebron. One of the most ancient cities in Israel, Hebron was significant in Jewish history as the resting place of Abraham and the patriarchs (Genesis 23:19). Though not a major location in Jesus' campaign, it was an important religious center during his time.

Jericho. An ancient city near the Jordan River, Jericho was where Jesus healed blind Bartimaeus (Mark 10:46–52) and where he met Zacchaeus, the tax collector who repented (Luke 19:1–10).

Jerusalem. The religious and political capital of Judea, Jerusalem was the center of Jewish worship and the location of the Temple. It was the site of Jesus' triumphal entry (Matthew 21:1–11), his final teachings, his arrest, trial, crucifixion, resurrection, and ascension.

Magdala. A town on the western shore of the Sea of Galilee, Magdala was likely the hometown of Mary Magdalene (Luke 8:2). It was a fishing center and a hub of trade.

Mount of Olives. A ridge east of Jerusalem, the Mount of Olives was a key location in Jesus' final days. He taught here (Matthew 24–25), prayed in Gethsemane before his arrest (Luke 22:39–46), and ascended from here after his resurrection (Acts 1:9–12).

Nain. A small village in Galilee where Jesus raised a widow's son from the dead, demonstrating his power over death (Luke 7:11–17).

Nazareth. Jesus' hometown in Galilee, where he spent his early years (Luke 2:39–40) and began his public teaching. He was rejected in Nazareth after proclaiming himself as the fulfillment of Isaiah's prophecy (Luke 4:16–30).

Perea. A region east of the Jordan River, Perea was under Herod Antipas' rule. Jesus spent time teaching and ministering there before heading to Jerusalem for the final time (Matthew 19:1, Mark 10:1).

Samaria. The central region between Galilee and Judea, Samaria was home to the Samaritans, a group with whom Jews had deep-seated animosity. Jesus deliberately ministered here, most notably with the Samaritan woman at the well (John 4:4–42) and in his parable of the Good Samaritan (Luke 10:25–37).

Sepphoris. A major city near Nazareth, Sepphoris was a center of Roman administration and culture in Galilee. Though not mentioned in the Gospels, Jesus likely would have been familiar with it, as it was a bustling city in his region. Some scholars speculate that Joseph and Jesus may have worked there as builders.

Shechem (Sychar?). A historic city in Samaria, Shechem was near the likely location of Jesus' encounter with the Samaritan woman at the well (John 4:5–26). It had deep religious significance in Israel's history.

Sidon. A Phoenician port city north of Galilee, Sidon was one of the few Gentile territories Jesus visited. He healed the daughter of a Syrophoenician woman here (Mark 7:24–30).

Tiberias. A major city on the Sea of Galilee, Tiberias was built by Herod Antipas and named after Emperor Tiberius. While it is not explicitly mentioned in the Gospels as a place Jesus visited, it was a key administrative and economic hub during his time.

Tyre. A Phoenician port city north of Galilee, Tyre was another Gentile region where Jesus ministered. He traveled here and healed a Syrophoenician woman's daughter (Mark 7:24–30).

Zebulun & Naphtali. Regions in Galilee where Jesus' early campaign fulfilled Isaiah's prophecy that a great light would come to those living in darkness (Matthew 4:12–16).

Jesus' campaign was not a collection of isolated events. It was a carefully orchestrated mission unfolding across first-century Israel. The accompanying map offers a geographical reference, highlighting key locations that shaped Jesus' mission. While it does not trace every movement, it provides a visual context for the world in which he operated, helping you to understand the terrain, political centers, and cultural settings that influenced Jesus' strategy.

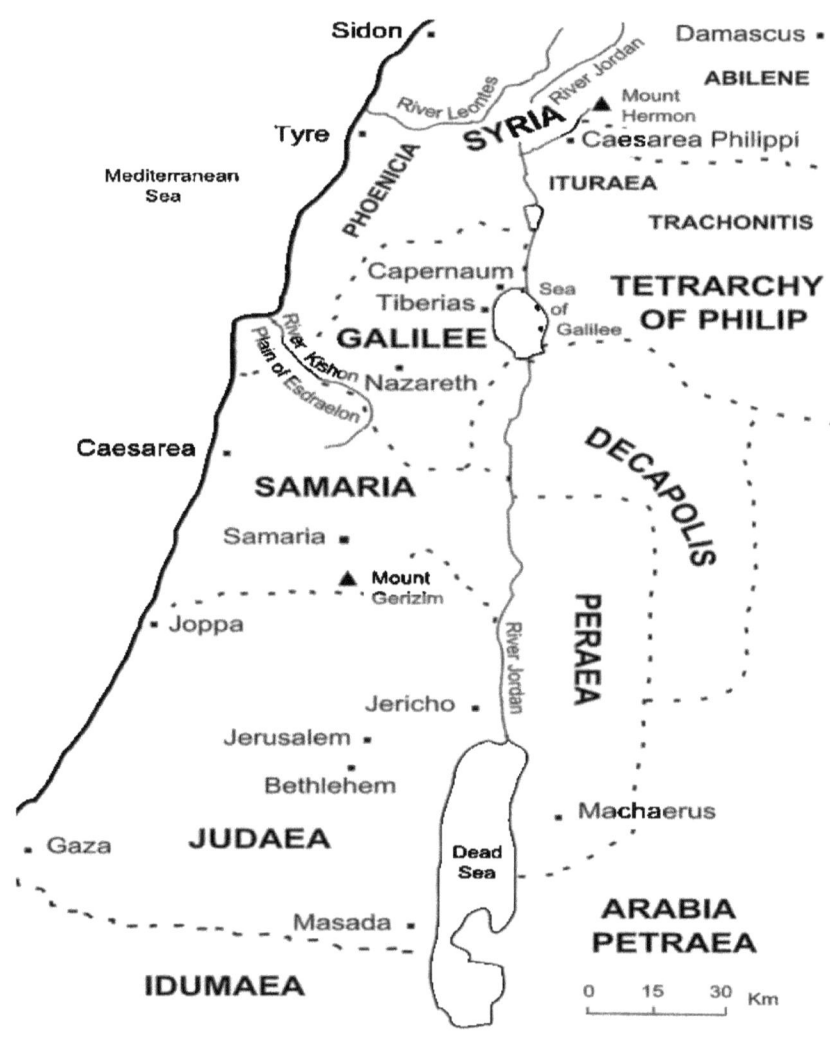

Allison, Dale C. Jr. *Constructing Jesus: Memory, Imagination, and History* (2010).

Boff, Leonardo. *Jesus Christ Liberator: A Critical Christology for Our Time* (1978).

Bornkamm, Günther. *Jesus of Nazareth* (1956).

Chancey, Mark A. *Greco-Roman Culture and the Galilee of Jesus* (2005).

Chancey, Mark A. *The Myth of a Gentile Galilee* (2002).

Crossan, John Dominic. *Excavating Jesus: Beneath the Stones, Behind the Texts* (2001, with Jonathan Reed).

Crossan, John Dominic. *Jesus: A Revolutionary Biography* (1994).

Crossan, John Dominic. *The Historical Jesus: The Life of a Mediterranean Jewish Peasant* (1991).

Dunn, James D.G. *Jesus Remembered* (2003).

Ellacuría, Ignacio & Jon Sobrino, eds. *Mysterium Liberationis: Fundamental Concepts of Liberation Theology* (1991).

Evans, Craig A. *Fabricating Jesus: How Modern Scholars Distort the Gospels* (2006).

Evans, Craig A., ed. *The Routledge Encyclopedia of the Historical Jesus* (2008).

Fiensy, David A. & James Riley Strange, eds. *Galilee in the Late Second Temple and Mishnaic Periods, Volume 1: Life, Culture, and Society* (2014).

Fiensy, David A. & James Riley Strange, eds. *Galilee in the Late Second Temple and Mishnaic Periods, Volume 2: The Archaeological Record from Cities, Towns, and Villages* (2015).

Fredriksen, Paula. *Jesus of Nazareth, King of the Jews* (1999).

Freyne, Seán. *Galilee from Alexander the Great to Hadrian: A Study of Second Temple Judaism* (1980).

Freyne, Seán. *Galilee, Jesus and the Gospels: Literary Approaches and Historical Investigations* (2000).

Green, Joel B., Jeannine K. Brown & Nicholas Perrin, eds. *IVP Dictionary of Jesus and the Gospels* (2nd ed., 2013).

Goodacre, Mark. *The Case Against Q: Studies in Markan Priority and the Synoptic Problem* (2002).

Goodacre, Mark. *The Synoptic Problem: A Way Through the Maze* (2001).

Goodacre, Mark. *Gospels before the Book* (2021).

Gutiérrez, Gustavo. *A Theology of Liberation* (1971).

Horbury, William. *Jewish Messianism and the Cult of Christ* (1998).

Horsley, Richard A. *Bandits, Prophets, and Messiahs: Popular Movements in the Time of Jesus* (1985).

Horsley, Richard A. *Galileans Under Jerusalem and Roman Rule* (2024, ed. K.C. Hanson).

Horsley, Richard A. *Jesus and Empire: The Kingdom of God and the New World Disorder* (2003).

Horsley, Richard A. *Jesus and the Politics of Roman Palestine* (2021).

Horsley, Richard A. *Jesus and the Spiral of Violence: Popular Jewish Resistance in Roman Palestine* (1987).

Horsley, Richard A. *The Prophet Jesus and the Renewal of Israel: Moving Beyond a Diversionary Debate* (2012).

Jeremias, Joachim. *Jerusalem in the Time of Jesus* (1969).

Jeremias, Joachim. *New Testament Theology: The Proclamation of Jesus* (1971).

Kloppenborg, John S. *Excavating Q: The History and Setting of the Sayings Gospel* (2000).

Lohfink, Gerhard. *Jesus and Community: The Social Dimension of Christian Faith* (1984).

Magness, Jodi. *The Archaeology of the Holy Land: From the Destruction of Solomon's Temple to the Muslim Conquest* (2012).

Magness, Jodi. *Stone and Dung, Oil and Spit: Jewish Daily Life in the Time of Jesus* (2011).

Malina, Bruce. *Social-Science Commentary on the Gospel of John* (1998, with Richard Rohrbaugh).

Malina, Bruce. *Social-Science Commentary on the Synoptic Gospels* (1992, with Richard Rohrbaugh).

Malina, Bruce. *Windows on the World of Jesus: Time Travel to Ancient Judea* (1993).

Meier, John P. *A Marginal Jew: Rethinking the Historical Jesus* (Vol. 1–5, 1991–2016).

Neyrey, Jerome. *Honor and Shame in the Gospel of Matthew* (1998).

Neyrey, Jerome. *The Gospel of John in Cultural and Rhetorical Perspective* (2009).

Neyrey, Jerome, ed. *The Social World of Luke-Acts: Models for Interpretation* (1991).

Pilch, John. *The Cultural World of Jesus* (Vols. 1–3, 1995–1999).

Putthoff, Tyson. *Jesus: The Strategic Life and Mission of the Messiah and His Movement—Volume 2: The Story* (2025).

Putthoff, Tyson. *Jesus: The Strategic Life and Mission of the Messiah and His Movement—Volume 3: Behind the Story* (2025).

Reed, Jonathan L. *The HarperCollins Visual Guide to the New Testament: What Archaeology Reveals about the First Christians* (2007).

Reed, Jonathan L. *Archaeology and the Galilean Jesus: A Re-examination of the Evidence* (2000).

Renan, Ernest. *The Life of Jesus* (1863).

Richardson, Peter. *Herod: King of the Jews and Friend of the Romans* (1999).

Richardson, Peter. *Building Jewish in the Roman East* (2004).

Robinson, James M., ed. *The New Quest for the Historical Jesus* (1959).

Safrai, Shmuel. *The Jewish People in the First Century: Historical Geography, Political History, Social, Cultural and Religious Life and Institutions* (1974).

Sanders, E.P. *Jesus and Judaism* (1985).

Sanders, E.P. *The Historical Figure of Jesus* (1993).

Schweitzer, Albert. *The Quest of the Historical Jesus* (1906).

Segundo, Juan Luis. *The Liberation of Theology* (1975).

Smallwood, E. Mary. *The Jews Under Roman Rule: From Pompey to Diocletian* (1976).

Sobrino, Jon. *Christology at the Crossroads: A Latin American Approach* (1978).

Strauss, David Friedrich. *The Life of Jesus, Critically Examined* (1835–1836).

Thomas, Robert L. & Stanley N. Gundry, eds. *The NIV Harmony of the Gospels, with Explanations and Essays* (1988).

Wright, N.T. *Jesus and the Victory of God* (1996).

Wright, N.T. *The Challenge of Jesus: Rediscovering Who Jesus Was and Is* (1999).

Wright, N.T. *The New Testament and the People of God* (1992).

Wright, N.T. *The Resurrection of the Son of God* (2003).

Wright, N.T. *The Day the Revolution Began: Reconsidering the Meaning of Jesus' Crucifixion* (2016).

www.ingramcontent.com/pod-product-compliance
Lightning Source LLC
Chambersburg PA
CBHW051637120626
46551CB00014B/2115